THRIVE

do more than
survive your faith

P9-DCU-875

Thrive
Do More Than Survive Your Faith

Copyright © 2011 Ben Hardman

group.com
simplyyouthministry.com

All rights reserved. No part of this book may be reproduced in any manner whatsoever without prior written permission from the publisher, except where noted in the text and in the case of brief quotations embodied in critical articles and reviews. For information, e-mail inforights@group.com, or go to group.com/permissions.

Credits
Author: Ben Hardman
Executive Developer: Nadim Najm
Chief Creative Officer: Joani Schultz
Copy Editor: Rob Cunningham
Cover Art and Production: Riley Hall and Veronica Lucas
Production Manager: DeAnne Lear

Unless otherwise indicated, all Scripture quotations are taken from the *Holy Bible*, New Living Translation, copyright © 1996, 2004, 2007. Used by permission of Tyndale House Publishers, Inc., Carol Stream, Illinois 60188. All rights reserved.

Scripture quotations marked MSG are taken from *The Message*. Copyright © 1993, 1994, 1995, 1996, 2000, 2001, 2002. Used by permission of NavPress Publishing Group.

Scripture quotations marked NIV are taken from *THE HOLY BIBLE, NEW INTERNATIONAL VERSION®, NIV®* Copyright © 1973, 1978, 1984, 2011 by Biblica, Inc.™ Used by permission. All rights reserved worldwide.

Scripture quotations marked NKJV are taken from the *New King James Version*. Copyright © 1982 by Thomas Nelson, Inc. Used by permission. All rights reserved.

Scripture quotations marked NRSV are taken from the *New Revised Standard Version Bible*, copyright 1989, Division of Christian Education of the National Council of the Churches of Christ in the United States of America. Used by permission. All rights reserved.

ISBN 978-0-7644-4809-6

10 9 8 7 6 5 4 3   20 19 18 17 16 15 14

Printed in the United States of America.

3 things

I really, really, really love my wife and my kids. They teach me every day, they give me hope, they love me when I am at my worst, and they believe in me infinitely more than I believe in myself.

I really, really, really love my church, The Avenue Christian Church (avechurch.com). There is no other family that I would want to journey with on the mission of God than you. I can't wait to see where God takes us and who he makes us to be on the way.

I really, really, really appreciate all of the spiritual guides who sat down with me when I was young and showed me the way. I can never repay you.

Ultimately, though, I am simply thankful that I am a child of God. I don't deserve to be a pastor. I don't deserve much of anything, but God has lavished his grace upon me! I pray that my whole existence is his!

For I decided that while I was with you I would forget everything except Jesus Christ, the one who was crucified (1 Corinthians 2:2).

Contributing Authors

Aaron Stern pastors theMILL, the college/20-somethings ministry at New Life Church in Colorado Springs, Colorado. He graduated from Oral Roberts University with a degree in business and later finished a graduate degree in theology. His first book (from David C Cook) will be coming out in spring 2011 about secrets and the power of confession. Aaron and his wife Jossie have four boys.

Andy Tilly serves on staff at Cross Timbers Community Church, a multi-site church based in the Dallas-Fort Worth area, as the executive pastor of family ministries. He also is the founder of the Xperience it! Foundation, through which he has authored three books and speaks at various camps, conferences, and faith-based events across the country.

Cam Huxford is the director of music, arts and productions at the Downtown Seattle Campus of Mars Hill Church. His alt-country roots-rock band, Ghost Ship, leads corporate worship gatherings and plays shows at bars and clubs in the Seattle area. Cam, his wife Hailey, and their new daughter Riley live in Seattle's Queen Anne neighborhood, where they enjoy tending their garden.

Dave Ferguson is a founding pastor of Community Christian Church and the visionary and movement leader for the NewThing Network. He is the co-author of *The Big Idea: Aligning the Ministries of Your Church Through Cooperative Collaboration* and *Exponential: How You and Your Friends Can Start a Missional Church Movement.* Check out the latest from Dave on his blog (daveferguson.org).

Jodi Hickerson and her husband, Mike, have been married and in ministry together for over 10 years. Jodi served as a teaching pastor and creative contributor at Heartland Community Church in Rockford, Illinois, for more than four years before moving to Ventura, California, to plant Mission Church. Jodi describes herself as a very grateful wife and mom (of three daughters), a crazy Kentucky Wildcats fan, and a believer that there is hope for everybody in Jesus Christ.

Jon Peacock worked for six years at Willow Creek Community Church in South Barrington, Illinois. Jon provided leadership to Axis, Willow Creek's young adult ministry. Currently Jon is the lead pastor at Mission Church, a brand-new church plant in the suburbs of Chicago. Jon brings a deep passion to unleash and empower the church to "be the church" in a world that desperately needs to experience the outrageous love of God.

Karl Halverson is currently the pastor of spiritual formation for The Avenue Christian Church, a new church plant in Louisville, Kentucky, reaching the university campus and old Louisville neighborhood. His experience includes 10 years of cross-cultural church planting in the Balkans (more than seven years living "on-field"), five years of youth ministry, and involvement in most facets of church life and leadership since Bible college and seminary. Karl has been married to Jill for over 17 years, and they have four really great kids!

Kyle Idleman is the teaching minister at Southeast Christian Church located in Louisville, Kentucky. He is the author and presenter of the award-winning video curriculum *H2O: A Journey of Faith* as well as *The Easter Experience* and *Not A Fan*. Kyle's favorite thing to do is hang out with the love of his life, DesiRae. They have been married for 15 years and have four children: MacKenzie, Morgan, Macy, and Kael.

Since 1990 Mark Moore has been a professor of New Testament at Ozark Christian College in Joplin, Missouri. In September 2008 he was awarded a Ph.D. from the University of Wales for his work on the politics of Jesus. Mark has authored more than a dozen books, mostly on the life of Christ (also Acts and Revelation). He is a speaker noted for his passion for the lost and his participation in completing the Great Commission of Christ. His life goal is to make Jesus famous. Mark and his wife Barbara live in Joplin.

Mike Filicicchia and his wife Jessie lead a house church full of ragamuffins in the finest dorm at the University of Michigan. He likes math and just recently learned how to write.

Mike Hickerson is the lead pastor of Mission Church (missionventura.com) in Ventura, California. Mike is a gifted leader and communicator and describes himself as a church planter, lucky husband, outnumbered dad (three daughters), Oklahoma Sooner fan, coffee addict, rookie golfer, and struggling surfer.

Steve Carter is an associate teaching pastor who now oversees the RockHarbor Fullerton campus in Southern California. He works with a great team of staff and volunteers who are committed to helping this young community become an actual family. Steve lives with his wife Sarah, their son Emerson, and their dog Fenway in Fullerton, California.

Contents

Contents

I've never written a book before, so when it was time for me to write an intro, I started looking at other books' introductions. I know that's lame and I probably should not admit that, but it's the truth. I drive a minivan and sing Thomas the Train® songs to my kids all the time, so I am fine with being called lame. If you are reading this introduction, you are probably already an overachiever; most people skip the intro and jump to the "good stuff." I usually skip them myself, but as I read these introductions I realized something: Each of the intros I read came with a promise. Some told me of how the book would change my life! Some told me of some secret knowledge I could find within the pages that would unlock some area of my life that I had never found before! Some promised growth, some promised knowledge, some promised peace, and some promised success!

I want you to know that this book doesn't come with a promise. In fact, it is written by a bunch of my friends who are very ordinary men and women. I love them and think they are very bright, but I think I speak for all of them when I say we really don't have any promises to make except maybe one! It's the thing that we all have in common, and it's one of the things that make each of these contributors my friends.

All of our lives have been changed by Jesus. All of our hope is found in him. The only promise we make is that you won't find anything life-changing in the devotional thoughts that await you unless you read them searching for him.

Our culture is filled with information about God. New books are published each day, books just like this one. We can download information at a faster pace than any other culture in the history of the world. Yet in the midst of all of this information, we lack transformation. In the middle of our learning, we aren't changing. The problem is we have been educated beyond our obedience and we have for way too long searched for a principle or a truth or an idea that will make our lives better, instead of searching for God.

I think sometimes we become the central figure of our faith! It's you! It's me!

The very first thing learned in Jewish culture by first-century Jewish children was the Shema:

"Listen, O Israel! The Lord is our God, the Lord alone. And you must love the Lord your God with all your heart, all your soul, and all your strength. And you must commit yourselves wholeheartedly to these commands that I am giving you today. Repeat them again and again to your children. Talk about them when you are at home and when you are on the road, when you are going to bed and when you are getting up. Tie them to your hands and wear them on your forehead as reminders. Write them on the doorposts of your house and on your gates" (Deuteronomy 6:4-9).

The very first thing we learn in our Christian culture?

The verse: *"For God loved the world so much that he gave his one and only Son, so that everyone who believes in him will not perish but have eternal life" (John 3:16).*

The song: *Jesus Loves Me.*

Can you see the slight difference?

Jesus does love us, with great deep affection, but he loves us for his glory and not for our own. He loves us so that he will be known, so that our very lives will proclaim his glory to the nations.

As Paul said:

Clearly, you are a letter from Christ showing the result of our ministry among you. This "letter" is written not with pen and ink, but with the Spirit of the living God. It is carved not on tablets of stone, but on human hearts (2 Corinthians 3:3).

And as Peter said:

And you are living stones that God is building into his spiritual temple. What's more, you are his holy priests. Through the mediation of Jesus Christ, you offer spiritual sacrifices that please God (1 Peter 2:5).

Let's be honest: We live in a me-first culture, and that attitude seeps into every area of our lives, including our learning, our attempts to grow, and our goal of living life to the fullest.

Paul says your life is God's letter to the nations; Peter says that our lives are monuments that point constantly to our great redeemer!

So here is my fear: I think you can read this book and find some new ideas, some new ways to look at Scripture, and some new learning to "show off" to your Bible study group next week. You may find some principles to help you get through the challenges of this week.

If that is what happens, you missed the point!

Our prayer is that in these pages you search for God—a God who is infinitely rediscoverable, a God who desires all of you, a God who not only loves you but also has a mission for you!

What we do promise is that God is worth it!

That God will change your life!

That in God you will find the answers!

So do me a quick favor—I know this may not be typical—but would you take a moment and pray before you read any further?

In fact, each day before you open these pages, would you ask God to reveal himself to you? Not so you can know more *about* God but so you can *know* God!

I'm not kidding; right now wherever you are, please spend a few moments asking the Holy Spirit to guide you, asking God to reveal himself to you, and asking God to change you not for your sake but for his!

The Gospels

Living Things Grow

My 4-year-old son never sleeps. His tiny body is full of energy, sweat, laughter, and pure innocence. Every night it's the same routine: We'll sing a song, read a story, say a prayer. We've tried everything, but as soon as I leave the room, I hear the Thomas the Train® theme being sung from his bedroom.

At least an hour will pass with no crying, no complaining—just the sounds of a young boy finding joy in life past his official bedtime. Eventually I go back into his room and sit on the edge of his bed. Oftentimes, I have to remove action figures and battery-operated toy cars from underneath his pillow. But this has become my favorite moment in the day because the conversations we have reflect an innocent heart and mind that is so precious to me.

We talk about the things little boys talk about: cars, wrestling moves, why we don't hit our brother, our love for ice cream, and sometimes even God. At the end of each of our talks, I tell him that I have a secret. I lean in close to his ear and wait for the silence to break with a little giggle. The waiting is worth it, because this is quite possibly my favorite sound in the entire world.

"I love you," I whisper to him. He giggles some more and then leans into my ear.

"I wuv you, too, daddy." He has a little trouble pronouncing the letter "L", which could be due to the fact that he's my only son born in Kentucky and has picked up a little Southern twang.

But soon, the whispering won't be as funny. The discussion on which superhero is best will have lost its intrigue. The Thomas® songs won't be as catchy (which wouldn't be THAT bad). The small little mispronunciations will be gone. And I'm beginning to mourn the fact that his sleepless nights will no longer be caused by an overflow of energy, but an awareness of the weight the world carries with it and his own experiences with pain and disappointment and heartache. It's not just about the late-night talks. It's the fact that I know he is turning into a "big boy"—a boy that will, before I know it, become a man. I pray that each step along the way, we will still have talks, even though the topics of discussion will change. But I will always remember my little boy who never wanted to sleep and whose lone act of defiance is humming a song about a blue train that fell off the track, when he's supposed to be sleeping.

The other day, with all of this on my mind, I simply asked him if he would stop growing for daddy. I told him I felt like he was getting too big and that I wanted him to be my little boy forever. He thought about it for a while, and then looked at me with a very solemn face.

"Daddy, living things have to grow!"

I'm not sure how my boy has grasped this early on in his life, but it's a profound truth. Maybe Dora the Explorer® taught him along with other important Spanish phrases like, "I love my backpack." Or maybe it's just instinct. Either way, the implications of this simple statement spoke to me.

I long for a living faith—a faith that inspires, a faith that calls others to action, a faith that challenges, a faith that breathes life into those around me. But there have been many days in my past when my faith has been, for lack of a better word, dead. There was no growth in my heart, no movement in my spirit toward loving God more, and no pouring out of love to those around me.

In Luke 13, Jesus is faced with a firestorm of tough questions about the news headlines during this time. In the middle of ritual sacrifices in the temple, Pilate had ordered his soldiers to take up arms and fight. To make matters worse, a tragedy happened as 18 people were killed when the tower of Siloam fell on them. People everywhere were wondering how to reconcile the brokenness and pain that come with this world. Jesus responded with these words:

"Do you think those Galileans were worse sinners than all the other people from Galilee?" Jesus asked. "Is that why they suffered? Not at all! And you will perish, too, unless you repent of your sins and turn to God. And what about the eighteen people who died when the tower in Siloam fell on them? Were they the worst sinners in Jerusalem? No, and I tell you again that unless you repent, you will perish, too" (Luke 13:2-5).

I think it's obvious that we live in a culture that demands answers to a world filled with hurt. Many times, people's questions are directed toward God, or a god of their choosing. Why do natural disasters happen? Why do good people suffer? Why can't everyone just get along?

This wasn't the first time Jesus spoke to the major social issues and tragic events of his time. Every time, there was a common theme: personal repentance. He points us back to our own hearts, to our own holiness, and to our own personal transformation—and he calls us to repent.

And in this, we see that Jesus was teaching us the reality that when the people of God fail to bear fruit, the world goes hungry. He knew the truth before my son did: that living things grow! Therefore, someone who isn't being transformed by his love and grace is, quite simply put, dead or dying.

Many of you live in communities that need God's restoration. You are surrounded by people who think that living is as simple as waking up in the morning and following what their hearts want. They are so busy chasing the American dream and living in the luxury of independence that they miss the reality of God's abundant life that he desires for each one of us. As a Christian, it can be overwhelming and often can lead to compromise or discouragement. In this, many students decide the grass is greener on the other side and enter into a place with so many rules that they lose their effectiveness in communicating with the world completely! Others compromise altogether and give up all God has for them, and they pursue a life of comfort and chase all the world has to offer.

But wherever you are, I think Jesus has one message for you: Change. Become. Obey. Follow. GROW. We are called to a living faith.

The next few pages will focus on the hope of the gospel, even when you are surrounded by broken and sinful people. Be encouraged that you have a Savior who knows your struggle as you learn to grow closer to him and breathe life on those around you.

by Mark E. Moore, Ph.D.

Jesus said a lot of important things, but he seldom said important things a lot. He just wasn't prone to repeat himself. Hence, when he does, we better have ears to hear. So here is his single most frequently cited saying: "If anyone wants to be my disciple, he must take up his cross and follow me."

We get that. Jesus calls us to a life of sacrifice. However, if you put on a yarmulke and listen as a first-century Jew, the terror of this saying becomes transparent. During the first half of the first century, the Jews lived under the oppressive domination of Rome. Though Jews previously had implemented crucifixion as a mechanism of social control, they weren't doing that during Jesus' day. They had lost legal jurisdiction. According to the Talmud, capital punishment had been stripped from the Jewish authorities just about the time Jesus began his ministry. Consequently, it was only the Romans doing the crucifying. Furthermore, Romans considered crucifixion so degrading that they banned crucifixion of their own citizens except in cases of extreme sedition. Bottom line: If you got crucified as a Jew, it was by Romans who considered you a debased beast deserving of the most humiliating death through excruciating torture.

So when Jesus invited his Jewish disciples to take up a cross, it was not an invitation to valiant sacrifice or noble service. It was an invitation to raw degradation, to abject failure, and to ultimate death. Taking up a cross was not giving up your rights or putting others first. It was not sacrificing your preferences or being willing to suffer. It was waving a white flag—an admission that you were a revolutionary who had failed in his vocation. This is hardly the kind of invitation that naturally would have swarming adherents.

For those of us who love the cross, who cherish it as a symbol of salvation, it is hard to hear with Jewish ears what Jesus' demand implies. That's because for us the cross of Christ is our means of salvation—a favor he did for us. It was that, indeed. But he didn't merely offer us his cross as a sacrifice for our sin. The cross is not a mere offer of forgiveness; it is a demanding way of life. Everyone who accepts the cross of Christ must also take up his own. The cross of Christ strapped to your own back is a lifestyle or, perhaps better put, a death-style. We don't merely receive the grace of Jesus through the cross; we submit to imitating his suffering and sacrifice. If you are not ready for that, Jesus says, "You cannot be my disciple."

Fast forward: What does this mean for a modern Christian? First, at bare minimum, it demands that we are revolutionaries. After all, those are the people who got themselves crucified. Jesus' movement was a full frontal assault on the systems of the world. It was a radical reconceptualization of what it meant to be Jewish. It was a complete rejection of the economic, military, and social machine of the Romans. Hence, for us, Christianity must also confront the systemic powers of our age. It is not a noble appendage we tack on to a balanced life so that we live symbiotically between work, leisure, and worship. It's not like a yoga class you take at the end of the day for health or stress relief. Christianity is a totalizing commitment to the kingdom of God. Though this has obvious implications for individual eternal salvation, there is no way to be an authentic Christian and not engage the world's systems that thwart the reign of God in the lives of those he so desperately loves.

Second, a cross-bearing life is an admission of defeat. This does not mean that we will fail in our revolutionary vocation. It means that the means of our victory will be through failure. Our self-denial and sacrifice is the mechanism of defeating Satan's agenda in our world. How does that work? Jesus explained it when James and John came and asked for seats of honor (Mark 10:35-45). They were bearing down hard on Jerusalem for what would be Jesus' final visit. They knew that their political agenda was coming to a head, and if Jesus pulled off the whole Messiah gig, there would be chief seats to be had. They asked for a pre-appointment to the highest administrative positions. The other disciples were livid, not because of their self-serving actions, but because the brothers beat them to the punch. Surely Peter had a thing or two to say about their claim to primary honors. One suspects that Simon the Zealot joined the chest-thumping and that Judas Iscariot put in his two cents' worth. They all wanted social significance.

Jesus' replay took their breath away, and we hardly understand it any better. He said, *"You know that those who are regarded as rulers of the Gentiles lord it over them, and their high officials exercise authority over them. Not so with you. Instead, whoever wants to become great among you must be your servant, and whoever wants to be first must be slave of all. For even the Son of Man did not come to be served, but to serve, and to give his life as a ransom for many"* (Mark 10:42-45 NIV).

There are two important observations that are not readily transparent in this passage. First, the high officials who "are regarded as rulers" literally means "regard themselves as rulers." That's a strange way of putting it, but the idea is that they give off the air of authority. Rightly so, actually. They have guards and garments that tell of their power. With a pass of their pen or an off-handed comment, the lives of their subjects can be tragically molested. Though their "underlings" do, indeed, recognize their authority, the impetus for leadership begins with the leaders who project themselves as important people.

The other important observation of this text is that the "rulers of the Gentiles" in the Gospel of Mark is a very shallow pool. Only two men fit that category: Herod and Pilate. Herod's tragic tale has already been told by Mark. He arrested John the Baptist at the prompting of his illicit witch of a wife and beheaded him against his own good sense due to the salacious dance of his teenage stepdaughter. In short, the dude got played! By whom? By his second wife and her junior high daughter. The audience is acutely aware of the irony: The ruler was ruled by his craving to be seen as a ruler. This is the inevitable truth of worldly rulers. The other Gentile ruler in Mark's Gospel didn't fare any better. Pilate, a known anti-Semite, got played by the chief priest, who deceived him into agreeing to a crucifixion he knew was unjust. How did that work? They blackmailed him. "If you don't crucify him," they said, "we will report that you are no friend of Caesar." The particular Caesar in view was Tiberias, the paranoid megalomaniac who had already assassinated Pilate's mentor, Sejanus. Pilate's future was in jeopardy and he knew it. So, in order to save a petty political career (which would end in exile in three short years), he washed his hands and threw in the towel. Again, the ruler was ruled by his desire to be seen as a ruler.

Jesus knows how this works in the world. If you want power, you are a slave to that lust. The only way to successfully carry out the kingdom of God is to abdicate worldly power and position. A cross strapped to your back is a shortcut to such a venture. Once you have shed all indications of self-protection and self-promotion, then there are no longer limits to your influence. Notice what Jesus said to his disciples: "If you want to be great, you must be the servant of all." That's what he meant by carrying a cross. Sometimes that results in literal death, but it always results in humiliation. It always results in association with sinners, and that is inevitably messy. But it also always results in honor in the kingdom. For when we serve the lowest on earth we attract attention of the highest in heaven.

Jesus never rebuked James and John for their desire to be significant. That drive may, in fact, be God-honoring. Rather, he gave them the shortest route to greatness in the kingdom. It is the heavy steps to the site of execution with a cross strapped to your back. Before you pick it up be warned: No one ever picked up a cross and then turned around to tell about it. This is a one-way journey with an inevitable end.

What have been the ways you have considered the cross and its place in your life with Christ?

How willing are you to fail, be degraded, and/or be humiliated in the worst ways possible for Christ's sake?

How have you let the safety of cultural, American Christianity define your life with Christ?

Has your life in Christ been defined by a search for social significance? If so, in what ways?

Do you agree with the last paragraph of this chapter? What will you do about it either way?

by Mark E. Moore, Ph.D.

There is a wonderful little figure of speech peppered through the pages of Scripture. It has a strange name: "epizeuxis." This is when a word is repeated for emphasis. Since the ancients didn't have word processors, epizeuxis was an effective way to emphasize their principal point. It sounds like this: *"Comfort, comfort my people" (Isaiah 40:1)*, or *"Fallen! Fallen is Babylon the great" (Revelation 14:8 NIV)*, or again *"Verily, Verily" (KJV)* in the Gospel of John, which the NLT simplifies to "I tell you the truth." You are going to run into an epizeuxis every now and again as you read your Bible, but very rarely will you ever find a triple epizeuxis. In fact, to my knowledge, there are only five in all of Scripture. This is like a double underline with bold red-letters in italics. Three are rather irrelevant for our present discussion (Jeremiah 7:4; Luke 13:33-34; Revelation 8:13). Two are of intense interest.

In 739 B.C. Isaiah had a vision of Yahweh. He was seated on his throne, high and majestic. The lower hem of his robe cascaded across the temple, and smoke careened through every crevasse. Seraphim flew overhead with a flaming radiance and with two extra sets of wings—one was used to hide their faces and the other their feet, for God's glory was too great even for them. Isaiah stood speechless amid their thunderous praise that shook the very portals of the temple; 24/7/365 they bellowed: *"Holy, holy, holy is the Lord of Heaven's Armies! The whole earth is filled with his glory!" (Isaiah 6:3)*. Their echo can be heard across the pages of Scripture until heaven is found opened again. In Revelation 4:8 the same angels sing the same song, declaring before the throne, *"Holy, holy, holy is the Lord God, the Almighty—the one who always was, who is, and who is still to come."* Twice we encounter this same triple epizeuxis: Holy, Holy, Holy. It bears repeating; it is that important. God is holy.

There are a thousand things that could be said of God. He is just, kind, creative, loving, wise, sovereign, omnipotent. As theological fancy ebbs and flows, various generations emphasize different attributes to God. Currently, our favorite seems to be "God is love." That's a good one, even a biblical one (1 John 4:8, 16). God is love—undeniably, irrevocably, incessantly. And fortuitously, this is a Christian message beloved by unbelievers. It is the very kind of preaching that resonates with the unredeemed who see in this attribute a license for lives lived in opposition to the commands of God.

Unfortunately, our emphasis of God's love often obscures many of his other biblical characteristics, including his holiness. What I'm saying is this: If we are going to be out of balance with any attribute of God, we should mimic the same imbalance of Scripture: God is Holy, Holy, Holy; Holy, Holy, Holy. God is never described as merciful, merciful, merciful, or patient, patient, patient, or even love, love, love. Each of these is true, but each does not carry the same emphasis from Scripture.

You would never know this by our preaching. In fact, in the face of a postmodern, politically correct culture, we wince when we hear a pastor preach on God's holiness. It smacks of judgmentalism or vindictiveness—a prudish kind of legalism with excessive demands to live according to antiquated moral standards. Granted, losing sight of God's grace is catastrophic. But is it really any better to lose sight of God's holiness? One cannot adequately teach John 3:16 without balancing it with John 3:18-19: *"There is no judgment against anyone who believes in him. But anyone who does not believe in him has already been judged for not believing in God's one and only Son. And the judgment is based on this fact: God's light came into the world, but people loved the darkness more than the light, for their actions were evil."* God's love is, indeed, open to the world but reserved for his elect. God loved the world so he gave his Son. Those who accept the Son are saved, loved, and protected. Those who reject the Son, however, have squandered their opportunity to experience the full and final love of God.

Let's be clear about holiness. It is not "holier than thou-ness." When the Scriptures speak of holiness, it is neither a list of rules to follow nor a catalog of worldly pleasures from which one must abstain. Holiness is not abstinence but devotion. The word itself implies that a person or an object is "set apart." Perhaps an example would help. A wedding dress is usually worn once. Why? Aside from the obvious physiological difficulty of sustaining the miniscule girth of a bride, the dress itself is devoted to a singular occasion. It's not designed for line dancing, barbecues, or shopping sprees at the mall. Likewise, your mother's china is "holy," devoted to Thanksgiving feasts and formal Christmas dinners. If she catches you warming up a Hot Pocket® in the microwave on her best china, you may experience the same shrill volume of the Seraphim in Isaiah's vision.

Personally, my toothbrush is "holy." I use it for but one thing and I alone have the prerogative to do so. My toothbrush, though perfect for the task, will never clean grout or scrub the back of the bathroom sink. Furthermore, after 26 years of marriage, my wife and I have shared virtually every physical thing, including colds and cupcakes—but never our toothbrushes. Medically, sharing a toothbrush is no more intimate than a decent kiss, but come on, it just ain't happenin' with my toothbrush! There are certain items that are special, so special that they are not to be shared. God himself is "set apart." There is no other creature on heaven or earth like God. None other can bear God's name or share God's glory. God is above and beyond, apart and distinct. In a word, God is "Holy, Holy, Holy."

When you give your life to God, he will set you apart from the world to be his exclusive property. You become God's bride, a betrothed one not to be shared. We are not talking here about piety. That is a kind of moral excellence that is attained through practiced abstinence. That has value, to be sure. But it is not holiness. Piety is what you achieve; holiness is what God declares.

Hear the parable of the symphony: In a symphony hall there are several seats of honor. One of them is on stage. It is where the first violinist sits. This individual is the single most important musician. She leads the tuning of all the other instruments, and she alone shakes hands with the conductor. She has earned that seat by years of diligent practice. You hear her play and you know this virtuosa belongs in that seat above all others. There is another seat in the balcony. It is perched high above the audience in a special box. This is where the royalty sits. For those in the box seats, there are no lines at the ticket booth or the concession stand. They have servants who open their doors and wait on them intently. When the concert is over, the conductor turns and looks above the crowd for the approval of the single figure in the center of the box. Surrounding the king is a court. They, too, have seats of honor, not because of any effort on their part, but because of their relationship with the king.

Most of us treat holiness as if it is the first chair of the orchestra. If we can just practice hard, giving up all other earthly pleasures, perhaps someday we can perform on stage and shake hands with the conductor. But God invites us into the box. God wants us to sit with him in relationship, not perform for him on stage. We seek the handshake of some conductor on stage and the approving applause of an audience. We should, rather, seek the higher chair, to sit with the king as part of his entourage, served by the conductor who used to be our master.

We are holy because God is holy, because he chose us to sit with him and to be part of his entourage. All he asks of us is that we dress appropriately in the clothes he provides. God's holiness makes us royalty; it behooves us to live accordingly. Yet ultimately, God is not interested in our performance so much as in our presence. Because God is distinctively holy, holy, holy, so too are we who have been marked by his Spirit and set apart as his people. *"You must be holy because I, the Lord, am holy. I have set you apart from all other people to be my very own"* (Leviticus 20:26).

At any point in your life, have you had a "triple emphasis" word from God for you? If so, consider its significance. If not, ask around among people to find out if they have.

Has the contemplation of God's holiness ever been a part of your relationship to him? If so, how has God worked in your life concerning his holiness? If not, start now to do so.

Can you put your finger on ways that God's holiness is expressed in your life or the life of your Christian community?

How have you defined holiness throughout your life in Christ?

What clothes are you wearing: rags of the world or the linen of holiness?

by Mark E. Moore, Ph.D.

The euphemisms we use indicate how insignificant we view our own sin. It's not adultery; it is an "affair." It's not a lie; it's a fib—or perhaps at most a "little white lie." We don't plagiarize, we copy; we don't slander, we gossip; we're not pornographers, we simply enjoy a little adult entertainment. Who are we kidding? Certainly not God. He has always taken sin seriously.

In fact, some of the examples in the Bible are downright frightening. Uzzah is a striking case in point. In an esoteric story from 2 Samuel 6, the priests were transporting the Ark of the Covenant back to Israel after it had been captured by the Philistines. God had told the Israelites back in Exodus 25:14 to carry the Ark by two poles slipped through the gold rings on each side. In this situation, however, the leaders decided to put it on an ox cart. After all, it was an awfully long way from Philistia to Israel. Well, somewhere along the journey, the ox stumbled; the cart tilted; the Ark slid precariously toward the edge of the cart. Uzzah reached out his hand to steady the Ark from falling to the ground and sustaining irreparable damage to this priceless artifact. In appreciation for Uzzah's concern for Yahweh's box, God smote him—a fine biblical way of saying, "Dude got whacked."

Earlier God killed an entire family for the sin of their father. His name was Achan, and during the conquest of Jericho, he conveniently retained a handful of silver, a gold wedge, and an expensive robe from the plunder that God ordered to be burned (see Joshua 6–7). Well, God inconveniently withheld his blessing from the troops, and on its next foray against a little 'burb called Ai, Israel got trounced, losing 36 soldiers, much courage, and most of its honor. Joshua, the commander-in-chief, complained to Yahweh, who informed him of the malfeasance. The consequence could not have been more severe. Achan, his wife, his children, his possessions—even his cattle, sheep, and donkeys—were stoned and then torched. Oy vey!

At this point, perhaps you are glad to serve the God of the New Testament? Surprise—he hasn't changed. In Acts 5, there is a terrifying tale of a couple that is sharply reminiscent of Achan. Their names were Ananias and Sapphira. In the early days of the church, people were selling property for the support of the poor. These two got in on the act. However, instead of giving the total proceeds of the sale, they only gave a portion. There's no real problem with that, except that they lied, saying they had given the full price of the sale so that they would receive the full praise from the congregation. When Peter questioned them (separately) about the offering, they lied individually. Consequently, they both dropped dead right there in church. Luke, in what can only be described as an "understated" comment, simply said this: *Great fear gripped the entire church and everyone else who heard what had happened (Acts 5:11).* Yeah, no kidding! If some dude drops dead for a little white lie, I'm buzzard bait!

This terrifying consequence for sin all started with Adam and Eve for eating a kumquat in Genesis 3. (So, you've heard it was an apple, but the Bible doesn't say so—OK, it doesn't say it was a kumquat either, but you gotta admit it makes the story more interesting.) Our initial response has to be, "Really? Death for a kumquat? Seems a bit steep."

These kinds of stories are Christian "contraband" kept hidden from our non-Christian friends lest they have extra ammunition against God as a vindictive dictator in the sky. What would they think about a God who executes capital punishment on seemingly minor offenses like lying, stealing, or touching a sacred object? This is, admittedly, a problem for those of us living in a culture that avoids the very word "sin." We make mistakes, we are "sick," we have problems, psychoses, and addictions, but "sin" is just not in our vocabulary. Nonetheless, if we are to be biblical people, we must think the thoughts of God, even about the uncomfortable topics like sin.

Here is a scriptural principle that should mark our minds: All sin is the sin of self, and that is mutiny against God. Scripturally, there are three categories of sin: The lust of the flesh, the lust of the eyes, and the boastful pride of life (1 John 2:16). These categories align with Jesus' own temptations in the wilderness. They also align with your experience with sin, and mine. All our transgressions fall into one of these three categories: physical sensations, covetousness, and pride. If that is not simple enough, each of these falls under a single banner—self. Bottom line: We sin because our "self" is on the throne. Theft happens because self wants something and doesn't care if it belongs to someone else. One commits adultery because that person craves attention and physical gratification, even at the expense of an unsuspecting spouse. Gluttony, rape, murder, lies, child molestation—every sin in Satan's arsenal overtakes us simply because and only when our self controls our soul.

Sin is a problem. What is the solution? The media suggest we indulge our self, obliterating the antiquated and offensive notion of sin. Mothers and psychologists suggest we love our self so we can become better people. Preachers and philosophers urge us to control our self and so withstand the onslaught of temptation. With all this sage advice, sin still spirals out of control. We need a better solution. The one offer from Jesus simply states, "Die to self"—take up a cross daily and imitate him. That, indeed, might work, for it addresses the primordial root of sin.

Why did Eve eat the forbidden fruit? It was not because she was famished. It was because she wanted to be like God. Why do we sin? For the self—the same reason. We want to be in control of our lives at the expense of everyone else in the universe, including Yahweh. The bald fact is that self is the source of sin, whether it is arrogance fed by self-adulation or a cutting disorder fueled by self-loathing. The root behind both evils is the sinful self that insatiably demands center stage. When that demand trespasses into the throne, it becomes a mutiny against God's divine majesty. Mutiny against God's righteous claim of lordship in our lives is the real issue behind every sin.

When we decry God's judgment, we ignore the underlying issue of our sin. "It was just a kumquat," we complain, "a little white lie…a tryst…an indiscretion." God's justice is neither fooled nor foiled by our vain attempts to justify our sustained mutiny against his divine prerogatives. Jesus understood that behind every foul word was a murderous heart too coward to actually pull the trigger (Matthew 5:22). Behind every lustful gaze lurks an adulterer too proud to commit an act that would tarnish his reputation (Matthew 5:28). Our deceit is an attempt to harness our wits for self-promotion or self-preservation (Matthew 5:33-37).

Our mutiny against God (let's call it what it is) really is that bad. Mutiny still is a capital offense. It jeopardizes the safety of an entire crew. In this instance, the mutual mutiny of humanity has created social systems that exploit the weak, domestic turmoil that preys on women and children, economic systems that engender greed, and political systems whose primary weapon is violence. We live in a world of sex trafficking and addictions, pillaging the earth and rabid isolationism, greed and racism. Why? Because our personal faults have excommunicated God from our world. It seems that our worst nightmare has come true: We asked God to leave us alone—and he did.

Just in case this secret does get out to your pre-believing friends, remember this: The penalty of the sin of self is death. And this God, so maligned for not intruding justice into our world, came to our space in the person of Jesus Christ. In his person, he absorbed our injustice in order that the righteous justice of God could be fulfilled. Or as one ancient saint put it: *Now, most people would not be willing to die for an upright person, though someone might perhaps be willing to die for a person who is especially good. But God showed his great love for us by sending Christ to die for us while we were still sinners (Romans 5:7-8).* This God, so maligned for being uncaring and vindictive, sacrificed his own Son for our sin. Hardly the brutal beast he is often portrayed to be.

P.S. There are two things that we, as fallen humans, almost always vastly underestimate: (1) The depth of our own depravity and (2) the depths to which Jesus descended to save us from ourselves.

What words do you have or use that "sugarcoat" sin?

What do you think about the idea that the OT and NT God is the same, especially when you consider his severity toward people at times?

Have you ever talked with your pre-Christian friends about the reality of sin?

How much of you, seriously, is at the center of your life?

How willing are you to make God through Christ the center of your reality, not just part of it and not just incorporated with it?

by Mark E. Moore, Ph.D.

This is simply stunning: The Greek word "grace" is found 155 times in the New Testament, but only 12 of these uses are in the Gospels, and most of these are in two brief passages (Luke 6:32-34 and John 1:14-17). We get a glimpse of coming attractions when John writes: *From his fullness we have all received, grace upon grace. The law indeed was given through Moses; grace and truth came through Jesus Christ (John 1:16-17 NRSV).* Generally, however, "grace" is not a concept that carried a lot of theological freight prior to Jesus' death. Outside the Bible, the word had been used as a kind of generic term for a gift given or a favor granted. In other words, Christians didn't adopt this word "grace" because of its deep theological meaning. Rather, they picked up a generic word for "gift" and impregnated it with incarnational theology. Mark this well: "Grace" is amazing because Jesus instilled the concept with the fullness of deity. This is a term that was created by the life and death of Jesus, not borrowed from any previous lexicon. Hence, in the Gospels, grace cannot be defined, merely described.

Grace showed up one cool morning following a night of passion. Snatched from her illicit lover's bed, she had been caught in a sting operation. They dragged her from an early-morning tryst across the dew of the temple pavement. With rough hands her judges cast her down to the cold stone pavement in front of the real target of their venom. She dared not look long at the stranger; even if she tried, she could not see clearly through bleary eyes filled with the tears of shame and betrayal. Nonetheless, her brief glance told her that this man was a peasant—simple but honest. This hardly bode well for her. What she needed in this moment was not an honest judge but something else—something mysterious and majestic, something other than justice.

Most of what was said was a blur. Her lover abandoned her and her dignity was stripped, so her mind was not quite clear. Yet she could hardly miss the first unmistakable thud from a sizeable stone hitting the ground. It wasn't long before the sound was repeated like popping corn in a frenzy. The next thing she heard was a gentle voice asking her a question that would mark the remainder of her days: "Where are your accusers?" She really didn't need his exhortation, "Go and sin no more." It wasn't so much that she had been caught; it was that she had been found—that is what changed her. She didn't know what to call it, there were no words for it; she simply knew that it felt like an embrace that was holy and right and good.

Grace showed up with a leper. He had been ostracized by his own, confined to a colony outside the city. His skin was infected with a curse that was highly contagious. It wasn't the medical problem that was most degrading but the isolation from his community and the heavy label he bore: sinner. He spent countless sleepless nights wrestling with God for an answer to a simple question: "What have I done to make you hate me?" And the heavens were silent. On that day, however, the teacher came to his little village. Before Jesus disappeared into the village, beyond the no-man's land where pariahs were permitted, our nameless leper confronted him. Forgetting himself, as well as the clearly defined boundaries proscribed by the law, he pleaded with Jesus, "If you are willing, you can make me clean." It is a mystery why this leper thought Jesus would be interested or able to heal him. In biblical literature and lore, only God healed lepers. Yet this man saw something in Jesus that made him take the risk. Other rabbis were known to repel lepers, even with stones! Yet Jesus had a different aura; he gave a different impression. The leper pleaded for healing; what he got was beyond all expectation. Jesus reached out and touched him. The leper had not felt a warm human hand on him since he first discovered his disease. In a world where contagion always passed from the unclean to the clean, Jesus reversed the order of the world so that his purity made that man clean. The disciples were aghast; the leper was healed. He didn't know what to call it, there was no word for it; he just knew that it felt like a spring rain washing him clean.

Grace showed up with a tax collector. He was despised, of course, mostly by the fishermen from whom he collected toll. He had a keen eye for those who attempted to sneak past his booth without paying their due. He had vicious bounty men who could enforce his sometimes-arbitrary assessments. He had a beautiful home built on the avarice of a Roman financial system that would have made Robin Hood quiver. He had lots of friends, bought with treasonous treasure. As the Master strolled the northern shore of the lake in Galilee, Levi was privy to his preaching. This taxman envied the fishermen from whom he extracted levy, and he secretly loved the ancient texts of Scripture. Never did he imagine that he could be a part of the kingdom of God, let alone be included in the intimate circle of Jesus' apostles. Yet one day Jesus stopped right in front of his booth. "Follow me," he said. There was no great fanfare and no special pleading. Just an invitation—a command really, couched in the fewest possible syllables. To the surprise of the crowd and the consternation of the disciples, Levi left his lucrative position on the spot. A party ensued. All his friends were invited, similar individuals of ill repute. It took Peter awhile to adjust, I'm sure, and Simon the Zealot likely never did. Matthew, however, was never the same. He didn't know what to call it. His superiors certainly had words for it that ought not to be repeated in polite company, but to Matthew, it felt like a clean slate.

Grace showed up on the darkest of days. Literally, the darkest, from noon until 3, as the sun refused to shine on three crosses bearing the bodies of two criminals and the one John described as "full of grace and truth." The chief priest orchestrated an assassination for the good of the nation. Pilate gave in. Judas betrayed. Peter denied. John fled. Mary wept. Jesus bled. Abandoned by friends, arrested by enemies, flogged to the bone, beaten beyond recognition, stripped in shame, pinned to a tree, mocked by the rabble, flanked by rebels, Jesus bled. It was the darkest of days. It was his turn to cry out to the heavens, "My God, My God, why have you forsaken me?" Then silence. If you can listen past the obscene mockery, hear underneath the wailing women, and pay attention to more than the tsk, tsking of the well-groomed religious elite, you can hear the garbled speech from parched lips, the most incredible sentence ever spoken. Surveying the hoards celebrating his death, the first thing Jesus said from the cross was this: "Father, forgive them for they know not what they do." I know these words, for I was there. If you also have ever stood at the foot of the cross, you know as well that there are no words in all the languages of humanity sufficient to describe what happened that dark day except this one single divine expression: "Grace."

Can you think of any "common" words in English that convey the truth of "grace"?

How have you understood grace throughout your walk with Christ?

How does grace reveal itself in and through your life?

What gift have you received that you hoped for but didn't expect to get and, in fact, didn't deserve?

What examples of God's grace have you seen in the lives of people around you?

by Dave Ferguson

What do you think is the most important skill for any relationship to be successful? Most people would probably say "communication." But it's always stuck with me what best-selling author Walter Wangerin Jr. says: "Communicating is *not* the most important relational skill. Forgiving is." If that is the case, and I believe it is, then all of us had better work at forgiving.

It's interesting that the word "forgive" in the original language of the New Testament literally means to "send away." That is exactly what I did with our trash last night: I "sent it away." I took it out to the curb so it could be hauled off. Every Wednesday morning I have a choice. I can either leave the trash around to clutter up and stink up the house, or I can "send it away." Those are the only two options. It is not going to go away or disappear on its own. I have to "send it away." And the longer I delay in "sending it away," the smellier and messier things become. The only way to get rid of the rotting, stinking clutter from past hurts and ruptured relationships is through forgiveness, through "sending them away." Working on forgiveness is the single most important key to having the kind of relationship that you want to have with whoever you are closest to.

One guy who knows much about forgiveness is Lewis Smedes. He says that in order to truly forgive, we need to know what forgiving is *not*. He wrote a chapter in one of his books called "Some nice things forgiving is *not*."

- Forgiving is not overlooking the wrong.

- Forgiving is not excusing or minimizing a wrong.

- Forgiving is not explaining things away to make it not seem so bad what somebody did to us.

That's not taking out the trash.

But here's the problem: Taking out the trash is relatively easy, isn't it? (Except when the bag breaks and everything dumps everywhere!) But forgiveness? Not so easy. In fact, someone once said, "Forgiveness is love's hardest work." But it may also be love's most important work. Here's why.

I heard a story about a hunter who was out hunting, and he came across the strangest thing: the skeleton of an eagle. Now, he'd seen animal skeletons before, but this skeleton had attached to its neck the skull of another skeleton. It was the skull of a weasel. And its jaws were clamped around that eagle's neck. The weasel's skull was all there was. Apparently they were both after some other animal, started fighting, and the weasel latched on to the eagle's neck and wouldn't let go. And the eagle apparently ate the weasel from the tail up to its head but couldn't reach the part of the weasel attached to its neck. The weasel never let go, and they both died. Gross, right? This reminds me of one of my favorite quotes from one of my favorite Christian writers, Frederick Buechner. He says:

> *Of the Seven Deadly Sins, anger is possibly the most fun. To lick your wounds, to smack your lips over grievances long past, to roll over your tongue the prospect of bitter confrontations still to come, to savor to the last toothsome morsel both the pain you are given and the pain you are giving back—in many ways it is a feast fit for a king. The chief drawback is that what you are wolfing down is yourself. The skeleton at the feast is you.*

Whether we're the eagle or the weasel and whether we started it or not, when we choose anger and animosity instead of forgiveness, we are the skeleton. When I'm harboring ill will against someone, most of the time it's not hurting that person; it's hurting me. Animosity is like hydrochloric acid, and your soul is not a container designed to hold it. It eats away at us. Hate always hurts the hater.

Did you know that non-forgiveness (aka "resentment") is actually intoxicating? Brain researchers tell us that resentful thoughts stimulate the pleasure centers of the brain, so animosity feels good at a biochemical level, but the cost is the eating away in your soul.

So if forgiveness is so hard and non-forgiveness feels so good, then where do we find the power to really forgive? We can start by learning it from a little girl.

In 1960, a 6-year-old girl walked into William Frantz Elementary School in New Orleans after a federal judge had ordered the desegregation of the city's public schools. The child's name was Ruby Bridges. As she walked in, a mob of angry white people, held back by National Guardsmen, called her names, yelled at her, and spit at her. Robert Coles, a child psychiatrist who later worked at Harvard, interviewed Ruby Bridges about it and asked, "When you were going through the crowd, people said your lips were moving. Were you talking back to the people?" Ruby said, "No." Coles asked, "What were you doing?" Ruby answered, "I was praying." Coles repeated, "Praying?" Ruby said, "Yes, usually I prayed before I got to the crowd of people, but that morning I forgot, so I prayed while I was walking in." Coles asked, "What did you pray, Ruby?" Ruby answered, "I was praying God would forgive them because that's what Jesus did on the cross." Soon after that interview, Coles committed his life to Christ. What Ruby said about Jesus affected his own soul.

We need to become people who can forgive like Ruby forgave, people who can forgive like Jesus forgave. And it all starts by accepting Jesus' forgiveness of us. *Make allowance for each other's faults, and forgive anyone who offends you. Remember, the Lord forgave you, so you must forgive others (Colossians 3:13).* God says to find in him our strength, reason, and motivation to forgive.

Remember that part of the Lord's Prayer that says, *"forgive us our sins, as we have forgiven those who sin against us" (Matthew 6:12)*? Have you ever prayed that? Have you ever meant it? Now think about this—what if

God answered that prayer? What if God said, "OK, you got it! I will forgive you just like you forgive others." Anyone up for that deal? Think about it! That's a pretty risky prayer.

And Jesus doesn't just stop there. Right after Jesus teaches his disciples how to pray, he says, *"if you refuse to forgive others, your Father will not forgive your sins" (Matthew 6:15).* I don't know about you, but I hear that and it makes me want to say, "Uh, God, you know that part about forgiving me like I forgive others? I take that back." The message to "forgive just as you've been forgiven" is repeated again and again throughout Scripture. But when we choose not to forgive, our relationships suffer and our relationship with God suffers. How messed up is it to think, "God forgives me of my sins against him, but I don't forgive that person of their sins against me?" My decision not to forgive somebody else makes my relationship with God out to be a sham. We say we can't stand hypocrites, but what is more hypocritical than *not* extending grace to someone when grace has been extended to us in such a lavish way? And just to be clear, Jesus is *not* saying that refusing to forgive someone is the unforgivable sin. He's *not* saying that unless you are perfect at forgiving everybody, God won't forgive you. What Jesus *is* doing is making a very important point: To *not* forgive somebody else is the most inauthentic, outrageous, dangerous, messed-up thing for someone who knows what it means to be forgiven by God. Jesus is using language to wake us up, shake us up, and help us grasp how incredibly messed up it is to *not* forgive people when we claim to be forgiven people ourselves.

So, if forgiveness is so important, how do we become better at it? We've all been told how to forgive: Say "I forgive you" and then never bring it up again.

The struggle isn't knowing what to do; the struggle is having the power and strength to do it over and over. Knowing what to do and being able to do it are two different things, aren't they? If I took you to a high school track and gave you the best running shoes and told you to run a 4-minute mile, could you? Doubtful. But what if I gave you a car; then could you travel a mile in 4 minutes? Things are different when you have the power to do them. What we need is *not* the simple mechanics of forgiveness; we need a source of power that helps us make it actually happen!

So we have to go back to the Resurrection. The fact that Jesus is risen and alive tells us he is *not* just a great example of forgiveness for us to try and imitate. The Apostle Paul says, *I also pray that you will understand the incredible greatness of God's power for us who believe him. This is the same mighty power that raised Christ from the dead and seated him in the place of honor at God's right hand in the heavenly realms (Ephesians 1:19-20).*

See, if the story ends with the Crucifixion, we just have the mechanics of forgiveness. We have Jesus' demonstration of how to forgive when we've been wronged. And that's important. But for most of us, because of the wrongs that have been done to us, an example to follow just isn't enough. We need something else beyond ourselves to empower us to forgive the way Jesus forgave. That is what the Resurrection promises us. This is the same mighty power that raised Christ from the dead.

How willing are you to forgive others (or to be forgiven by others)?

What definition of "forgiving" have you used throughout your life?

Are there any people whom you resent? Why do you resent them?

Have you ever connected the distance you feel from God to your unwillingness to forgive others?

If forgiveness is about Christ's power in our lives to walk as he walked, are you letting him or believing him to be that power? Why or why not?

Journeying With God

Taking What Isn't Mine

About two years ago, we began a process to adopt a little girl from Ethiopia—a long process full of joy and pain, heartbreak and celebration. A year into the process, we received our first pictures of her. Her name was Tarike Abdela, and when she joined our family it would become Claire Tarike Hardman. We fell in love immediately, we bought baby clothes, we prepared a nursery, and we loaded ourselves up with trinkets and reminders of her home.

We waited until the day came, and we celebrated the good news of our daughter with all of our friends. The night we heard the news that she was our daughter, we went to the local Ethiopian restaurant with friends and celebrated together. Although Ethiopian food is not my top choice, we still had a great time, celebrating and thanking God for the new gift in our family. Then the call came, telling us she was not officially our daughter. Apparently, there were problems, our case would go before a judge again, and it was likely that she would not be our daughter.

You see, about five years ago, my wife Sarah was diagnosed with Obsessive Compulsive Disorder and began taking medication to treat the problem. It was fairly serious for us at the time, but thanks to medication and treatment, it has not been an issue for many years. In fact, she only sees the doctor once a year now. Of course, all of this is on our official report to the Ethiopian government, and for some reason it scared them. Someone somewhere objected to our adoption, and for months we went into a period of waiting that included 22 court dates that would most likely change our lives forever. Forget the money invested in the adoption, the years of praying, and waiting; the reality was that we believed God had asked us to adopt, and every step along the way we had done our best to be faithful. It was hard to imagine what would happen if the court said no—if I would never hold my little girl, if the clothes we bought were never worn, and if the very pink empty room in our home would never be filled with the laughter of our baby girl.

It seems to me that my biggest challenge recently is taking what isn't mine. I'm always doing it. I play God! I steal his role, I want to play his part, I want to be in his seat. I want to tell God how it should be, how this should work out. I readily want to follow God on my terms, and I am quick to doubt and question whenever things go wrong. I move into fear—fear for my daughter, fear for my wife, fear for my family, most of all fear that I am not in control. I move into why mode—why would this happen, why is this so hard, why aren't we receiving any good news? I want so badly for her to be my child that I forget that she is God's child. I want so badly to take what isn't mine.

I don't simply mean it's all about this little girl; it's so much more than this. I want to carry the weight of my life, sometimes the weight of the world. I want to fix it myself; I want to control it; I want to chart out the plan, work toward it, and make it happen. The problem is, it isn't mine—no matter how heart-invested I am, no matter how sincere my faith is. There are these moments when I simply need to let God be God and stop taking his role in my life.

So in this process I don't really know what my posture with God should be. There has been some begging and pleading, there has been some cursing and shouting, and there has been a quiet surrender. Mostly, I am simply giving it all back: all the weight I carry that isn't mine, all the problems I try to solve on my own as if I do ministry for Jesus, instead of him doing ministry through me. I'm giving back my money, my possessions, my future, my dreams, my plans, and my baby girl, and I am speaking clearly, "These things never belonged to me, they are yours. Long ago I gave my life to you and everything in it. I guess it's time for me to really start living like it belongs to you."

"For I hold you by your right hand—I, the Lord your God. And I say to you, 'Don't be afraid. I am here to help you. Though you are a lowly worm, O Jacob, don't be afraid, people of Israel, for I will help you. I am the Lord, your Redeemer. I am the Holy One of Israel' " (Isaiah 41:13-14).

We live in a culture that says we should attempt by all means to elevate ourselves—a culture where we believe by the sheer power of our will we can achieve, we can succeed, and we can overcome all obstacles. Ralph Waldo Emerson once wrote, "Trust thyself, every heart vibrates to that iron string. Discontent is the want of self-reliance. It is infirmity of will." "Trust yourself" seems to be the tagline of our existence these days, so the phrase "you are a lowly worm" doesn't sit well with us. In fact, we have a very tough time humbling ourselves enough to know and understand how God is full of such grace and mercy that he would ever call us his children at all.

We all love pride, we all love self-exaltation, we all love our own abilities, and sometimes we believe in ourselves more than we believe in God! So in this text from Isaiah 41, we are reminded that we must acknowledge our pride. We must acknowledge that we are afraid, that we want to control things, that we want to do things on our own, and that we want to take what isn't ours. Not only should we acknowledge it, but we also should ask God to take our hands, ask him to take our fears, and ask him to show us how small we are!

Charles Spurgeon said, "I can only turn to my comrades in arms, in the good war of Christ, and say to them, brethren, you and I can do nothing of ourselves; but let us dare great things, for God will not leave us."

So come now long expected one with healing in your wings, come and take what belongs to you and teach us to become fully surrendered to the joy and pain of following you. May we enter into the joy with hearts on fire and a voice to tell the world, and may we walk through the pain with a quiet confidence of knowing you are there as well. May we know that everything is yours, the ups and downs, the joys and the pains, and everything in between. May I find myself in surrender, may I know you more through the pain, and may I one day no longer desire to take what is yours. Until then grant us peace!

The following pages are about our simple, day-to-day journey with God. Our prayer is that they provide wisdom on how to move from being like the world and trusting in ourselves, to being like Jesus and trusting fully in him.

by Andy Tilly

Growing up, I heard several phrases over and over. They went like this: "Andy, let's go, time for church," or "You're going to make us late again, and God doesn't like tardy people!" Perhaps my favorite one was "You cannot wear that to church." I heard that one almost every Sunday. I could never understand why full camouflage and a fake army knife weren't OK for a nice church gathering. It wasn't like the camouflage was going to hide me as I stood beside the purple banner that read "Jehovah El Shaddai," which means "God Almighty."

But seriously, church has always been a huge part of my life. From the Bible Bowls to getting the little gold star for memorizing John 3:16, I ate it up. Like many people, I attended weekly and knew a lot of facts and stories. I also had a healthy amount of fear that if I did anything wrong, God was waiting to bring down his vengeance upon me.

Unfortunately, there was a major problem. Even though I knew the stories and facts, what to do and what not to do, most of the time I still did whatever I wanted—until later in life, when one chapter of Scripture changed everything for me. I found it when I was older and had moved out of my parents' house.

I picked up a very, very dusty Bible. I have heard it said that "dusty Bibles lead to dirty lives," and perhaps that is true, but at the time, I was just getting ready to play a little game I like to call Bible Roulette. Maybe you've played it before. If not, let me give you the lowdown. It goes something like this: You're not sure where to start reading, so you flip through the Bible, praying that God stops your hands at just the right place.

Normally, Bible Roulette doesn't work for me. In fact, I'm pretty sure Bible Roulette rarely works for anyone, but thankfully, on that day, things were different. Of course, you tell me whether or not I really won the game. Clearly, what God had in store for me that day was a little brutal.

I started in James with some great encouragement that went like this. *If you need wisdom, ask our generous God, and he will give it to you. He will not rebuke you for asking (James 1:5).*

I can use some more wisdom, I thought. I was only one minute into this game, and I already liked what I was hearing. However, that quickly transformed into conviction. James turned on me. Suddenly, it hit me with being slow to speak and not becoming angry! Not easy for someone as high-strung and vocal as I was. Then the knockout passage came out of nowhere. It shook me to the core.

But don't just listen to God's word. You must do what it says. Otherwise, you are only fooling yourselves. For if you listen to the word and don't obey, it is like glancing at your face in a mirror. You see yourself, walk away, and forget what you look like. But if you look carefully into the perfect law that sets you free, and if you do what it says and don't forget what you heard, then God will bless you for doing it (James 1:22-25).

The first two sentences of that passage say almost everything there is to say about being a follower of Jesus. They made me look at my life. Hard. Listening to the Word was something I had done for years. That was the easy part, but there was something else that I didn't know about. I was deceiving myself. I was full of information and low on doing what the information said. Huge problem. And I know I am not alone. It happened all throughout the Bible.

In Matthew, Jesus called out some people who knew Scripture better than any of us: the Pharisees and teachers of the law. Now, I know they get a bad rap, but understand that they devoted their lives to memorizing Scripture. They spent more time studying the Bible in one year than most of us do in a decade. These guys were the experts. And while people respected them, Jesus was about to mix it up.

Then Jesus said to the crowds and to his disciples, "The teachers of religious law and the Pharisees are the official interpreters of the law of Moses. So practice and obey whatever they tell you, but don't follow their example. For they don't practice what they teach. They crush people with unbearable religious demands and never lift a finger to ease the burden. Everything they do is for show. On their arms they wear extra wide prayer boxes with Scripture verses inside, and they wear robes with extra long tassels" (Matthew 23:1-5).

That is not what I would want to hear come out of Jesus' mouth about me, but Jesus was making a point. And he makes the same point today.

Did you catch it? These guys knew what to do. They were great listeners, but they were deceived because they didn't live out the knowledge they had in their heads. I had the same problem.

Several things came into focus for me that day. First, I realized that God really isn't interested in the plethora of knowledge we have if we don't live it. I always thought that the more I knew, the happier God would be. Now I understand that knowledge must lead to action or it's wasted.

The second thing I did that morning was to ask myself some hard questions. The issue wasn't whether or not anything needed to change in my life; it was how much and how fast. I had to make changes. They didn't happen all at once, but God always gives plenty of grace and mercy through the changing process. I discovered that by cleaning up my life and getting rid of the junk, I inevitably drew closer to God. The more I listened and applied what I knew, the better my life became. It's a truth I discovered through that process, and it's a truth that still applies today. Life goes so much better, and I stay out of a lot of trouble, when I listen to and obey the Word of God.

How about you? Is there something in your life that is contrary to God's Word? Is it a dating relationship that started out healthy but now involves spending the night? Is it the absence of daily disciplines for a follower of

Jesus like praying, reading, or serving? Maybe it's an addiction that you need broken or a habit that could kill you.

Maybe you're like me. Maybe you don't have to look very far to discover places where you have been listening to the Word but not doing it. Ask yourself the tough questions today. Stop saying, "I will change tomorrow," or worse, "It isn't that big of a deal." You can be sure that if you ask God what in your life needs to go and what areas have been invaded by sin, he won't be shy about telling you. And when God tells you, listen! Make it easy on yourself and just *do it*!

five questions

In what ways are you still doing what you want and not what God wants?

What "knockout" verse, if any, has God used to radically change your life?

In what ways have you not only been "hearing" what God has said but also "doing" what he says? In what ways haven't you been?

How often do you ask others to "do as you say but not as you do"?

What things do you know are true but are unwilling to live out?

by Aaron Stern

My wife Jossie and I have four kids—four boys to be exact: Parker, Cohen, Brooks, and Smith. As a result, our house is testosterone central. For us, excitement around the house means black eyes, Spider-Man® Band-Aids®, basketball competitions, wrestling matches, and even the arrival of a fire truck after someone has fallen on his head—which has happened twice! There is never a shortage of activity, and we have more than enough roughhousing to go around.

People often ask, "Are you going to try and have a girl?" While I understand the question, it is an awkward one for me. You see, at one time we were going to have a baby girl and we lost her.

After three boys, Jossie and I found out that our fourth child was a girl. We were to have a princess in the house with a bunch of older brothers. Everything was normal until week 32. A routine doctor's visit turned out to be anything but routine when the doctor became very concerned because our little girl's organs were surrounded by fluid. We were rushed to a hospital in Denver for tests and evaluation, and 24 hours later we found ourselves driving back home to Colorado Springs trying to process a long list of potential health problems for our little girl. We soon found out that the chances for her survival were minimal; even if she made it to delivery, she would only live for a few minutes.

Exactly two weeks later, we went to the hospital because Jossie hadn't felt any movement in her belly all day. Our little princess had died. We were in shock as a dream shattered before our eyes.

I had not really experienced tragedy in my life prior to the loss of our daughter. My grandparents died at old ages, and although a car hit the family dog, for the most part things had gone "the way they are supposed to." This loss destroyed that pattern. I'd cherished dreams of walking my daughter down the aisle, but instead I found myself standing at a grave, putting her in the ground, and picking out a headstone. It wasn't the way things were supposed to be!

I was devastated. The pain of loss was piercing. My world was spinning and turned upside down, and I didn't know which way was up. The grief was overwhelming. I had never known what it was to weep, to question, or to get knocked down like this.

Some years later, I can say that there is hope after grief, yet I also know that it isn't time that heals, but the journey that happens within that time. If we let him, God will accompany us on a journey down a road that leads from lament to hope.

Understanding trouble and pain is the first step in this journey. Our culture says life should be convenient and comfortable, and in many ways, American Christianity has bought into this worldview. This consumer-driven gospel teaches that walking with God is all about us as God meets our needs and makes our lives better. It completely disregards the words of Jesus in John 16:33 when he explains, *"Here on earth you will have many trials and sorrows."* Our tendency is to jump to the next phrase: *"But take heart, because I have overcome the world."* There is ultimate victory in Jesus, but it doesn't discount the fact that we as Christians will face trouble. It may not be a loss of a child for you but the loss of a job, the diagnosis of a disease, the ending of a marriage, the death of a loved one, or the betrayal of a friend. Difficulty isn't just a possibility; it is a promise given to us by Jesus. I am still looking for a plaque that would go above a doorframe with this promise on it—similar to the "You will be blessed in your going in and going out." The more I realize that I am not immune to pain and difficulty as a follower of Christ, the greater my chance of moving toward hope.

In my grief and suffering, I found myself drawn to Job and was struck by two things early on in the book: first, how absolutely terrible he had it (if you are ever having a bad day, read the book of Job and chances are your difficulty won't seem so bad); and second, how Job 1:20 says that *Job stood up and tore his robe in grief. Then he shaved his head and fell to the ground to worship.* Job's first response was worship. This worship response did not stem from having all the answers—we know he had lots of questions, and the rest of the book is packed full of questions and wonderings—but Job responds with worship. We might not understand and might hate what is happening to us or around us, but acknowledging that God is still God and choosing to declare his greatness and goodness are powerful places to start.

The book of Psalms is filled with chapters of praise, adoration, and encouragement, but I was surprised to discover that two-thirds of the psalms are laments. David and the other writers cry out to God with great passion, bemoaning that they feel alone, abandoned, or rejected. In my laments I have found great solace in praying the psalms. I used to approach Psalms from an intellectual perspective, focusing on things like the circumstances of David's life when he wrote a particular psalm. However, in the season of grief that followed the loss of my baby girl, I began to approach the psalms from an emotional perspective, letting them engage my heart. I let my heart cry in the way that David and others had so many generations before. But I didn't stop there; I was also careful to ensure that my heart landed in the same place that David's did:

O Lord, how long will you forget me? Forever? How long will you look the other way? How long must I struggle with anguish in my soul, with sorrow in my heart every day? How long will my enemy have the upper hand? … But I trust in your unfailing love. I will rejoice because you have rescued me. I will sing to the Lord because he is good to me (Psalm 13:1-2, 5-6).

Psalms give words to my feelings, and they also direct my heart toward the truth.

If the sorrow expressed throughout the book of Psalms isn't enough to believe that laments are a part of our lives, consider the fact that an entire book of the Bible is named after them. Lamentations was likely written by the prophet Jeremiah as he mourned the desolation brought on Jerusalem and the Holy Land by the Chaldeans. Lamentations is written as an acrostic, meaning that each verse in the first four chapters begins with a letter of the Hebrew alphabet taken in order. The Jews used the book of Lamentations as a symbol of walking through grief step-by-step. In other words, grief isn't just something that melts away after time, but a process that God works in and through. God intends for us to walk through pain instead of just sitting in it and enduring it until it is gone.

Walking through this process demonstrates our trust in God, our trust that Jesus has done all to makes things right. This hope is ultimately what allows us to move from lament to a place of true healing. This hope seems to be shattered all of the time here on earth. I know that I have often asked God, "Why didn't you fix this?" The answer to that question is simple: "I have." In the death and resurrection of Jesus we experience the complete remaking of all things in the end. Living with this perspective allows us to live for so much more than ourselves, because we know that everything that is broken now will be made whole someday. We don't engage God looking to see what he can do for us, but with an eternal perspective that looks to fit into his greater story and purpose.

It is in Jesus, his work on the cross, his coming out of the grave, and our experience of heaven that God makes all things right. It is true that there are a lot of things on this earth that aren't as they are supposed to be, but we can live confident lives in Christ, truly experiencing both the pains and the joys of this world because we know that they will all be set right in the end.

Have you ever known what it is like to "weep and mourn"? What was it like?

How has your perception of life reflected the attitude that "life should be convenient and comfortable"?

What are your normal responses to difficulty in your life?

If you've ever felt "abandoned by God," did you pursue him in the midst of that situation? If not, what did you do?

What place do the realities of Jesus' life have in the difficulties of your life?

by Mike Filicicchia

"So what are you all about?" The question seemed to simultaneously hit me across the face and suck every ounce of breath out of my lungs. "What have I gotten myself into?" I wondered to myself as I sat there across a cafeteria table from my new small group leader. His name was Kyle, and he was a fourth-year political science major who was already slightly balding, played guitar like a pro, and would be planning his wedding by the end of the school year. And apparently he asked really intense questions, too (as if he wasn't already a daunting conglomeration of everything intimidating to me as an 18-year-old). I was just a few weeks into my freshman year at the University of Michigan and was completely unacquainted with the concept of an older guy being genuinely interested in learning more about me. I racked my brain for an impressive response.

Nothing.

Hard as I tried, I found myself unable to offer a life thesis that sounded even halfway put-together. No one had ever asked me a question remotely like it; I felt wildly unprepared for both the depth of the question and the offer of relational intimacy it placed before me. "What am I all about?" I wondered. I mean, there are things I like to do and people I like to be around. I felt like maybe that should count for an answer. But Kyle's question assumed something much deeper about me: that I actually had a mission, a purpose in life. And even worse, it assumed that I had some idea of what it was.

I didn't know it at the time, but I needed his question. I needed someone to give me permission to go below the surface of my life, and I needed someone I could trust to help me navigate those uncharted waters. Sure, I had been in church small groups in high school, where this kind of help was theoretically available to me, but I never quite trusted that someone would truly care or would help me without judging me. Nobody asked me questions like Kyle's, so I shared just enough to get by. As a result, the deepest parts of me remained completely isolated from human contact, and I suffered from a loneliness that had become so familiar that I didn't even know it qualified as loneliness.

I thought it was just what it meant to be human.

That was until a very well-timed question, anyway. Kyle invited me into authentic relationship, and I took him up on the offer. I've been a staunch believer in the power of a great question ever since.

I'm convinced that great questions are at the very center of God's tactical method to win our hearts. Consider a classic Jesus scene (Luke 18:18-30): A rich ruler comes to Jesus, calling him "Good Teacher" and asking what he needs to do to inherit eternal life. Jesus, knowing that this man's allegiance rests with his wealth and not with God, asks him, "Why do you call me good?"

Pause here.

Now put yourself in the other guy's shoes. You just realized that Jesus has left you with two options: You can either blushingly rescind the title you just gave this man, or you can acknowledge his divinity, thus leaving yourself completely vulnerable to whatever he might then ask of you. You know you'd feel foolish for calling him God and then shrinking back from his response (you've followed all the religious rules your whole life). But inwardly you tremble at what you sense to be true: that this man knows you perfectly and possesses the power to expose the deepest purposes of your heart, meaning he may very well call you to repent of that other god you've been worshipping—your riches. Both prospects are terrifying.

Though good advice lies deep within the heart, a person with understanding will draw it out (Proverbs 20:5). Jesus possessed perfect insight and understanding, and he was always masterfully drawing out the depths of the human heart with his questions. When speaking with the rich ruler, Jesus leverages a timely question to hold up a mirror for the soul. He does the same with Simon Peter in John 21, echoing that haunting refrain, "Do you love me?" And elsewhere, as his disciples discuss the latest theories of his identity, Jesus halts the conversation and asks them point-blank, "But what about you? Who do you say that I am?"

Jesus asked this question uniquely to each and every person he encountered. In all situations, he could instantly rip past spiritual games and personal masks to hold up a soul mirror in the form of a question that somehow asked, "Where are your allegiances right now? What god are you actually serving?" It was the last question most people wanted him to ask—the one that blatantly yet gently exposed the deepest desires and intentions of their hearts, the objects of their greatest affections. They felt utterly exposed yet neither condemned nor humiliated because he didn't live to shame them. He was actually offering a choice: persistence in idolatry, leading to corruption and death; or a new path of repentance leading to freedom and life.

And he's offering you that same choice: a choice between freedom and slavery, between life and death.

To live a life choosing truth and repentance is costly, but to reject it is to kill that essential part of you that longs for a life of epic adventure immersed in a life-or-death battle between good and evil. To continue your life in a spiritual fog, soothed and numbed by ignorance, is eternally more costly, but its comfort and familiarity can make it seem as though nothing is at stake.

I know God is asking you this because he's always been doing it. God has hotly pursued humanity, cutting through our fogs and vying for our hearts through penetrating questions, for as long as humanity has existed. Even in the very beginning, when our relationship with God was first broken, when God first needed to come searching for us, his first interaction after the Fall was—you guessed it—a question. ("Where are you?") This gentle yet revealing response to humanity's blatant betrayal gives us incredible insight into the character of God. His words weren't what most of us might expect, having grown up in a broken world where our wrongdoing is often ignored, rejected, or condemned. God was wooing them into relationship, into romance, acting as their fierce Pursuer. He didn't do so with force but with an invitation to reconciliation in the form of a question. It's absolutely incredible.

Even more incredibly, God actually wants you and me to be the ones who extend his invitations, to act as his ambassadors. He trusts us that much. You and I live in a fallen world where we're surrounded by people who desperately need reconciled relationships with God. As we embody the Pursuer heart of God in this world and learn to ask his questions, we can actually extend God's invitation into relational depth and intimacy to everyone we know. Do you feel unworthy yet?

But before you strap on your world-changer boots and walk out the door ready to ask the perfect questions to everyone you meet, you must know one thing: This all starts with you. The person most in need of some spiritual re-evaluation right now is you. It's always you. I don't say that because you're particularly degenerate, but because it is the constant scheme of Satan to lead us into believing that the real problem rests with the "other person." All of us can find someone who needs more spiritual fixing-up than we do, so Satan tempts us to occupy ourselves with pointing the finger and thinking about how to fix the other person rather than evaluating our own heart.

If you will make it a practice to constantly ask God to hold up the mirror in your own life and ask other God-honoring people to act as a spiritual mirror for you, God will honor your lifestyle of honesty and repentance by moving in your life in ways you never thought imaginable.

My friendship with Kyle continues to be a source of spiritual rejuvenation for me. His continued questions and presence in my life are powerful because he listens attentively to the Spirit of our Pursuer God and simply verbalizes what God is already asking me. Those questions change my life because they lift sin's fog in my life, revealing the reality of my spiritual condition, but also because they remind me that I'm worth being pursued; that there is a passionate Savior who's always seeking after me. God is wooing me—and you—into deeper relationship through his questions. So make this the day when you declare to God that you're opening a two-way street of questions between you and him.

What questions could you ask God to grow your relationship with him? You can find some great ones in the book of Psalms, or try a few of these:

- What were you saying to me in the midst of that tragedy?

- Why do I continually struggle with this sin?

- What step of faith are you calling me to take right now?

- How do you want me to love the people around me?

- How can I most glorify you with my life?

God also has gentle, pointed questions for you. What's the last question you want God to ask you right now? (Remember, you don't have to fear God's questions because there is no condemnation for those who are in Christ. If you confess your sin, he is faithful and just and will forgive and purify you completely.) Maybe you sense God asking you questions like these:

- Who or what are you blaming?

- Where have you been turning when you feel lonely?

- What do you long for more than anything else right now?

- Would you follow me even if it meant losing _____?

I hope that through these questions you begin a journey of taking God's hand and exploring the deepest parts of you. There is no reason to fear what you might find because God promises to cleanse it all as white as snow. I pray that you would be someone who forever hears, heeds, and repeats the questions of our great Pursuer God.

by Andy Tilly

Michael is a friend of mine who attends the University of North Texas. Over the last several years, I have really gotten to know him and his family. Michael has been a follower of Christ for about 10 years, and it shows in almost everything he does. He seems to make the right choices and avoids the traps of the freedom-at-college lifestyle. He serves within his community, studies Scripture, and leads a small group.

Now if it sounds like I am making him out to be as perfect as Jesus, I assure you he's not. Michael is, however, obedient. He knows what is right and wrong and tries his very best to obey God's Word.

But does his obedience make him dependent on God? That's a huge question.

How do you move from simply doing what God says to living a life that is totally dependent on God?

My friend comes from a wealthy family where college, cars, and a place to stay aren't even a consideration. While most people get student loans, grants, or scholarships, Michael doesn't even know what those applications look like. It goes without saying: His family is blessed.

Knowing I was going to be writing on this subject, I recently asked him, "What are you depending on God for?"

He stood puzzled for a few seconds and then gave the classic answer: "*Everything!*"

I laughed out loud and said, "Nice try. Really, what are you depending on God for?

A few more seconds of silence, and then the truth came out: "Nothing, I guess."

Ouch!

Here was a great guy who was doing all the right stuff, but when it came down to it, because all his physical and material needs were met and life was perfect, he wasn't depending on God for anything. Yes, Michael was obedient, but he wasn't dependent.

So how do we make the transition? First, we must understand that these two things go together. Obedience is a huge part of depending on God, because often in the midst of desperation, obedience is what will get you through the tough times.

Michael is a great guy, and it won't be long before he truly becomes dependent on God. He is on the right path, and true obedience leads to dependence. Look at the life of David. In 1 Samuel 16, Samuel was about to anoint the next king. The person he chose was the most unlikely one: a shepherd.

Then Samuel asked, "Are these all the sons you have?" "There is still the youngest," Jesse replied. "But he's out in the fields watching the sheep and goats." "Send for him at once," Samuel said. "We will not sit down to eat until he arrives." So Jesse sent for him. He was dark and handsome, with beautiful eyes. And the Lord said, "This is the one; anoint him." So as David stood there among his brothers, Samuel took the flask of olive oil he had brought and anointed David with the oil. And the Spirit of the Lord came powerfully upon David from that day on. Then Samuel returned to Ramah (1 Samuel 16:11-13).

David accepted the anointing, and who wouldn't? We don't know for a fact that David or his family realized exactly why the prophet was there that day; the passage doesn't indicate if Samuel fully explained the purpose of his visit. But as we continue reading through 1 Samuel, we learn that David was obedient many times over to God and the king, Saul. Soon, though, David found himself in a place where obedience and dependence collided!

In 1 Samuel 17, David took on Goliath. You've heard the story. The best part of the story came at the end: *So David triumphed over the Philistine with only a sling and a stone, for he had no sword. Then David ran over and pulled Goliath's sword from its sheath. David used it to kill him and cut off his head (1 Samuel 17:50-51).*

If only we could do that to bullies today! (Just kidding! But as the guy who was the smallest kid in the class, maybe I'm not kidding!) David became an instant celebrity with the people, and they chanted his name through the streets.

King Saul wasn't very happy about this. David was gaining popularity and doing everything he was supposed to do, yet Saul's jealousy was about the make the obedient David dependent. By 1 Samuel 19, Saul was trying to kill David. He had the power, money, and people to do it. He could do what he wanted; he was the king. David went on the run and continued to escape with help from God and from Saul's son, Jonathan. Later in his life, David became king, and we can read about his dependence in the psalms he wrote, including this one:

I wait quietly before God, for my victory comes from him. He alone is my rock and my salvation, my fortress where I will never be shaken. So many enemies against one man—all of them trying to kill me. To them I'm just a broken-down wall or a tottering fence. They plan to topple me from my high position. They delight in telling lies about me. They praise me to my face but curse me in their hearts. (Interlude) Let all that I am wait quietly before God, for my hope is in him. He alone is my rock and my salvation, my fortress where I will not be shaken. My victory and honor come from God alone. He is my refuge, a rock where no enemy can reach me. O my people, trust in him at all times. Pour out your heart to him, for God is our refuge. (Interlude) Common people are as worthless as a puff of wind, and the powerful are not what they appear to be. If you weigh them on the scales, together they are lighter than a breath of air. Don't make your living by extortion or put your hope in stealing. And if your wealth increases, don't make it the center of your life. God has spoken plainly, and I have heard it many times: Power, O God, belongs to you; unfailing love, O Lord, is yours. Surely you repay all people according to what they have done (Psalm 62:1-12).

David's obedience led him to a dependence on God! When you and I follow God's voice and call, we will encounter times when we cannot control the situation or circumstances. In those moments, our dependence and faith in God are all we have. And truthfully, that is all we need.

Now I'm asking you: What are you depending on God for? You could say, "life," "air to breathe," or "not getting hit by a bus," but really—what is it that you are looking for God to do within your life that only he can do? Is it to open doors for you, supply the money to live out your dream, or speak clear direction for your life? Is it to deliver you from a sickness, or bring the right marriage partner to you? No matter what it is, I can tell you with certainty: Your obedience today will lead to total dependence tomorrow.

Enjoy the journey!

five questions

In what ways are you not only obedient to God but also dependent on God?

Think of different times you've had to depend on God; what did these times look like, or how did they make you feel?

Have you ever experienced a time when obedience and dependence collided? What did you do?

In what ways have the wrong actions of others forced you to depend on God?

Are you willing to totally depend on God? Why or why not?

Idolatry

My Fake Real Girlfriend

"For my people have done two evil things: They have abandoned me—the fountain of living water. And they have dug for themselves cracked cisterns that can hold no water at all!" (Jeremiah 2:13).

We met on a weekend church retreat to southern Indiana. I somehow ended up in the same car as her. We both knew it wasn't by chance; we had our eye on each other for some time: the tiny glances across the room during the Bible study, the quick eye contact, and the even quicker "playing it cool" when I was caught looking. The lingering after meetings simply for a conversation about nothing. Church retreats can escalate relationships tenfold, so one day at a church event with a girl is like 10 days in the real world. Maybe it's the constant singing of slow songs, the moonlit gatherings, the campfires, or just simply the fact that nearly every man at a Bible college is looking for a wife and nearly every woman at a Bible college is looking for a minister husband. Whatever it was, we knew after the weekend and the four-hour drive home that we were a couple.

We did what couples do. I called; we talked. She called; we talked longer. We went out, we ate food, we laughed, we watched movies, we kissed. When you're 20 and lonely, and when your parents were junior high school sweethearts and have told the story over and over again, you can end up feeling like love should be coming soon. So I jumped in, I took it to the next level, I defined the relationship, and I told her I was not going to date anyone but her—something that I already wasn't doing, but by saying it, everything was more official. Then we talked a little more, ate a little more together, watched a few more movies, and kissed a little more. We were a real couple; the campus was abuzz. When I say it was "abuzz," I mean some guy from my dorm my freshman year asked me if we were dating and one of her friends told me we were a good couple, but I was sure the campus was buzzing with the news of our relationship.

My heart somehow got ahead of my mind, and very quickly she became "the one." But I realized it wasn't going well. I knew that she wasn't kind to me. I noticed she started calling less, and then we ate less food, watched fewer movies, and kissed less. I tried to focus more of our attention on the kissing, but she was suddenly busy with school and classes and grades—things I rarely acknowledged and things that would never have gotten in my way of kissing.

She told her economics class she was single, which confused me because she wasn't single and because who she was dating had nothing to do with the social science of the production and consumption of goods and services. She was named the queen of the campus at homecoming, but I wasn't king; I wasn't even one of the guys who wears a suit and walks around the track next to the king. I imagine I landed somewhere in the middle, definitely not a king but also not a pauper or a regular townsman. I was probably like an ironworker or a cupbearer—something pretty important but just not the king. I'm not sure being the king or queen of a Christian college was something anyone should be proud of anyway.

We would walk through campus and she stopped holding my hand. She stopped really caring. She was just there, and so was I.

The question I always ask myself: Why did I stay?

I think I liked the thought of being in love so much that I wanted to believe it could happen, that it already had happened. So I followed her around for months. I took tiny abuses each week, nothing severe enough for me to believe it was over and nothing serious enough for my not-really-real relationship to end but enough for me to begin thinking:

"Hmmm, I wonder if every guy's girlfriend refuses to talk to him when they go to parties together? I wonder if everyone's girlfriend doesn't call him back for days at a time? I wonder if everyone's girlfriend seems to enjoy the attention from most of the other guys on campus and not enjoy the attention from the person who is allegedly her boyfriend?"

So the night finally came, on the front porch swing, when she told me she didn't love me anymore. I'm fairly certain she never did. But I was convinced that I loved her. I drove home to Ohio. I stayed in bed for a day. I thought about dating lots of other girls over the next few months to make her jealous—so I went on two dates in six months.

I hated myself and was miserable for weeks, not because I missed her, although at the time I thought I did, but I was really miserable because I had failed. Because the thing I had been chasing wasn't real. Because what I had wanted so badly was still out of my reach.

Sometimes we want to be somewhere so badly that even when we know in our hearts we aren't there, we pretend that we are.

So many times in my life I've chased the dream of what I thought was real and felt exactly the same as I did on that porch that night. We do it every day: We choose the created things over our Creator; we choose an idol over God. We choose what is fake instead of what is real. All the while, we know in our hearts it will disappoint, but for some reason we stay.

We stay in the relationship. We stay in the job. We stay with the career path. We stay with the same belief system. We stay when we know we should leave.

We stay because we simply want to believe that we have captured what is real.

So we chase our idols. We chase our careers. We chase our cars. We chase our prestige. We chase our success. We even chase bad relationships.

We dig and dig and dig, even though we know in our hearts that we are digging in vain and we know that at the end of all the digging, all we will have is a big hole.

But we ultimately realize what we knew all along—that this isn't real!

A few years after this breakup, I met my wife, and she always held my hand in public, she liked eating food with me, watching movies with me, and kissing me, and if by chance the topic of our relationship were to come up in her economics class, she proudly would have claimed me. She talked to me at parties and wanted to be with me all the time. I quickly realized what a relationship really looked like and what real love was.

It wasn't so hard. It wasn't so tough. It was real!

Very quickly all of my past relationships just seemed silly. They didn't matter because I had found what was real.

I once was a fool in love. In love not just with a girl who didn't love me but in love with a world that had nothing to offer me. I chased after all it offered to give. I chased success, I chased prestige, I chased money and fame, and I found in the end that it wasn't real! Then I met Jesus and my life drastically changed. I realized that what I wanted I found in him: acceptance, love, hope, peace, and joy all wrapped up in my identity as his child. They say an infant can't really know himself or herself outside of a mother's gaze. I honestly believe that we can never truly know ourselves outside of Jesus. We find ourselves wrapped up in idolatry when we choose anything from the world to try to satisfy a part of our being that was uniquely designed to be satisfied by God!

Where in your life are you chasing an idol?

Where are you pursuing something that isn't real?

The next few pages are all about what happens when we choose something from this world to try to satisfy a part of us that can only be satisfied by God. It's dangerous and it's everywhere around us, but there is hope!

by Cam Huxford

"Should I bow down to worship a piece of wood?" (Isaiah 44:19).

The prophet Isaiah tells a story of a man who goes into the forest and cuts down a cedar tree. He chops up the tree and brings home the wood. As the story goes, he uses half of the freshly chopped wood to build a fire for cooking his food, but then after dinner he takes the rest of the wood and builds an idol out of it. When he's done, he falls down and starts to worship it. He prays to his leftover firewood. *"Rescue me!" he says. "You are my god!" (Isaiah 44:17).*

That story is heartbreaking. But it's not unlike my own. My good friend Mike built my guitar. Ten years ago he built it out of a solid piece of mahogany. He gave it to me, and I played it for years. I used it as a tool for leading corporate worship gatherings, and I loved it. But one day I noticed myself looking down at this block of wood, this mahogany board, and saying, "You will deliver me. Music will deliver me from obscurity by helping me gain exposure and prestige. It will deliver me from a sense of worthlessness by giving me an identity. Music will deliver me from poverty by helping me make a living. Music will be my god." I made music my God for years.

Isaiah responds to such foolishness with this: *How foolish are those who manufacture idols. These prized objects are really worthless. The people who worship idols don't know this, so they are all put to shame. Who but a fool would make his own god—an idol that cannot help him one bit? All who worship idols will be disgraced along with all these craftsmen—mere humans—who claim they can make a god. They may all stand together, but they will stand in terror and shame (Isaiah 44:9-11).*

I've seen Isaiah's words prove true. God has put me to shame. After years of my foolish, shameful, wicked idolatry, by his overwhelming grace, God crushed that idol and continues to crush it every day. But here is what is amazing to me. He didn't just crush it and take music out of my life. He crushes it and redeems it for his glory. For the past few weeks, when our band is together backstage before the service, we've been thanking God in our prayers that he allows us to use music to worship him, when we've been guilty of using it to worship ourselves. God lets us worship him with the very thing we once worshipped.

This story about a man worshipping a block of wood comes from Isaiah 44. Here's how that chapter ends. God says to his foolish, wicked, idolatrous people:

"Pay attention, O Jacob, for you are my servant, O Israel. I, the Lord, made you, and I will not forget you. I have swept away your sins like a cloud. I have scattered your offenses like the morning mist. Oh, return to me, for I have paid the price to set you free" (Isaiah 44:21-22).

So, how can you dismantle a god?

What does Isaiah 44:22 mean for me day-to-day as I attempt to lead worship in spite of my still idolatrous heart? What does it look like to return to the one true God because he has redeemed me? It seems like every day I want to build something new to worship. I find something else that might deliver me. Surely something my hands can make will deliver me from the mess my hands have made.

A more recent example is my current struggle with fear of man. I can become a real people-pleaser at work and begin to think that my deliverance from financial destitution hinges on my ability to impress my boss. How do I know if I'm impressing him? Well, by adding up all the good feedback I get from him and writing it in the left column in my Moleskine® in black ink, subtracting the number of times I get reamed by him, which of course is written on the right column in red ink, and celebrating the surplus of good works. Sounds ridiculous, I'm sure. This game can get pretty nasty real quick.

The good news is that idol crushing starts with God. He's been dismantling false gods through all of history. God has done everything from raining down fire on altars to Baal, to toppling Asherah poles, to digesting golden calves, to turning over money tables in the temple, and he's still at work crushing idols today. Isaiah 44:11 promises that God will put all our idols to shame together.

An amazing example of this comes to mind, an example that involves an altar to Baal. I had the opportunity to lead worship at the seminary I attend on a day John Piper was going to be in attendance. I thought to myself the day before, "You know what? I am going to impress this guy." So I spent some time that evening writing out what I would say between each song, thinking that Pastor John would be really impressed with my ability to cram two mini-sermons into a 15-minute worship set. The next morning, God gave me a vision. The reason I know it was from God is because it was an image directly from Scripture. The picture was of Mount Carmel. On top of it stood 450 prophets of the false god Baal and one prophet of the one true God, Yahweh. I realized this was a scene from 1 Kings 18. Because I've always thought of my role as a worship leader to be a prophetic role, my first thought was, "I'm just like Elijah, the one true prophet of the one true God. God is affirming my deft ability to lead worship." However, then by a miracle, I saw myself in the vision and I wasn't Elijah, but rather I was among the 450 prophets of Baal. That's when it hit me. I am just as false a god as Baal ever was, and I'm trying to convince people to worship me. How dare I stand on a stage and use music and parlor tricks to pedal a false god.

Isaiah 44:23 says this: *Sing, O heavens, for the Lord has done this wondrous thing.* The Lord, the one true God, conquers false gods. Verse 22 tells us that God blots out our sins like a cloud and crushes our sins to mist. As he breaks down our idols, he beckons to us, "Return to me, for I have redeemed you." God is not only the great idol crusher but also the great idol redeemer. With the many times I've used the role of worship leader to pedal a false god, has he taken that role away? No! God has redeemed me and redeemed even my idol as a platform in which I could point to his greatness in my exposed brokenness. If you want practical advice on how to dismantle a god, here it is: Return to the one true God because he's already done it. Stop trying to worship the splinters of a god he's already crushed.

five questions

Where do you find your identity?

Can you put your finger on some ways God is calling you to find your identity in him?

How willing are you to let God smash your idols? How willing are you to get rid of the splinters?

What are your favorite "parlor tricks" to use in getting people to worship you?

Can you identify any ways in your life that God is redeeming you even though you have worshipped idols?

by Aaron Stern

When we read the Scriptures we can see quickly and clearly a dominant and recurring theme: God is interested in our lives belonging completely to him.

The first of the Ten Commandments says that no other gods are to come before him. Of the many kings that led the nations of Israel and Judah, the wholehearted were honored by God, but those whose hearts were divided missed out on his blessing. Jesus reiterates the high value that God places on wholehearted devotion in the Great Commandment: *"The most important commandment is this: 'Listen, O Israel! The Lord our God is the one and only Lord. And you must love the Lord your God with all your heart, all your soul, all your mind, and all your strength' " (Mark 12:30).* In Revelation, John commends the church at Philadelphia for its faithful devotion while the church at Laodicea is rebuked for being lukewarm in its love for God.

God expects undivided devotion from his people. God wants to be first. In Exodus 20:5, God says that he is a jealous God, meaning that he isn't willing to share the affection that he alone deserves. (That idea is echoed elsewhere in Scripture, too.) The best way for me to understand this jealousy it to think about the love and devotion I have for my wife and my expectation that she will reciprocate. If some guy were to come on the scene and try to flirt with my wife or somehow intrude on our commitment to one another, a holy jealousy would rise up within me. There is no room for another person in our marriage; in the same way, there isn't any room in our relationship with God for another.

The kings who gave less than their all did not reject the One True God, but they did add gods like Baal from surrounding nations to their worship. One of the reasons they did this was to appease the other nations. How often do we do something in "worship" for the benefit of someone other than God, something that is more about appeasing their expectations than communicating our total love and adoration for our Savior and King? These kings practiced syncretism, adding other gods to the mix. We may not reject God but instead add him to the portfolio of gods in our heart. We communicate that God is important, but a few other things share his level of importance in our lives.

When God isn't first, everything that comes before him is an idol. God doesn't want any idols in our lives. When I think of an idol, the first thing that comes to mind is some statue of a fat, pot-bellied man or a crazy-looking creature with snakes coming out if its head carved out of stone, whittled out of wood, or shaped out of metal. So if someone were to ask if you have any idols in your life, you would probably quickly respond no. Not so fast! It is important not to dismiss the question simply because we don't have anything in our house with incense burning next to it. We can easily read the story of Moses receiving the Ten Commandments at Mount Sinai and think that Aaron and the Israelites were clueless when they formed a golden calf while they could see the smoke at the top where Moses was meeting with God and receiving the law in written form. We, of course, would never do that. Yet we are just like the Israelites. We might not be melting our jewelry down, but just as an idol can be easily created with our hands, so too can we easily create an idol in our hearts—one that is often harder to detect, especially when couched in religious terminology.

Tim Keller, an author and the pastor of Redeemer Presbyterian Church in Manhattan, says our hearts are idol factories. I like this phrase because it highlights the efficiency with which we create idols. It's not just something that is easy for us, but it also is something that happens with regularity. Because we have an incredible capacity to build idols, the hunt to find them and the steps to tear them down must be continuous and focused.

Idols can be obviously bad like greed, power, or revenge, but really anything can become an idol. Idols can begin as good things that are turned into ultimate things. It's not that we can't love things a lot; in fact, we are meant to love and enjoy them, but they are never meant to take the place of God or hold the same significance as God in our lives.

Family, money, possessions, career, or good grades all can become idols. A girlfriend or boyfriend can become an idol. It is OK to have a significant other, but that person becomes an idol when he or she takes the place of God and pulls devotion that belongs to him.

What may easily go undetected and slip under the "idol radar" are not just good things but spiritual things. Have you ever thought that church, your close group of friends, or the Bible could become an idol? What about worshipping the experience of worship more than worshipping Jesus, or chasing a good band and a good speaker more than the living God, or giving greater devotion and commitment to your church than to Christ?

This can happen in a lot of different ways, but I actually believe that in church, it is often even easier for good things to become idols. Maybe you always have a smile on your face because you want to show God's love to others. That's a good thing, right? But what if the real issue is that you don't want people to know that you aren't perfect, that you don't have it all together? Maybe pride couched as evangelism has become your idol. Perhaps you spend every evening volunteering at the church but neglect to spend time with your own family. What if meetings, volunteering, and the spiritual high you feel at church have become idols in your life? Is it possible that we can miss Jesus all in the name of Jesus?

Obviously, you and I aren't interested in missing Jesus, right? Because idols are so easily created, I find it helpful to ask myself the following questions on a regular basis. I know some people who've written them in the front of their Bibles to serve as a consistent reminder to check their priorities and make sure that God is first.

How do I spend money?
Jesus frequently taught about money and possessions, including this verse: *"No one can serve two masters. For you will hate one and love the other; you will be devoted to one and despise the other. You cannot serve both God and money" (Luke 16:13).* Follow your money and you will find out what is in your heart.

How would I respond if things in my life were taken away from me?

The next time your computer crashes, you don't get the grade you wanted, your phone deletes your contact list, you lose your job, or you open the fridge to discover there's no more Mountain Dew®, use that time to evaluate your response. It is OK for something to be important enough to make you feel sad if you lose it, but would you lose your will to live? Do you feel yourself freaking out just at the thought of losing a prized possession?

Where am I finding happiness, security and significance, or fulfillment?

It is so tempting to find these things in people—parents, friends, spouses, bosses, or pastors—but nobody other than God can truly provide any of those results. Even though you need other people in your life, anything you receive from people is a cheap substitute for the wholeness you will find when you place God above everything else in your life.

Finally, I think it is important to specifically identify if spiritual things have taken God's place: Have I experienced and do I continue to experience God firsthand, or am I living off someone else's leadership, support, or experiences?

Depending on your answers to those questions, it may be time to get rid of some idols. Our first response at finding that something has taken the place of God should be repentance.

Our second response should be our decision to get to know God in a way so that we recognize that he is everything we need. If you need money to feel secure, a title to feel significant, or a church service every night to feel holy, search the Scriptures to learn what God has to say about those things. God's Word is living and active and is the most powerful tool we have when it comes to tearing down idols. Your life will be richer when you keep God at the center of your life, but the real reason for making that decision is because God deserves it.

Can you think of any ways that your heart is divided regarding God-honoring things?

What are some practical and beneficial implications of God's jealousy for you?

What idols does your "idol factory" produce?

Read through 1 and 2 Kings; which king are you most like in faithfulness to God?

Sit down in silence, with everything turned off. Consider your heart. What is taking the place of God in your heart?

by Cam Huxford

I thank whatever gods may be
For my unconquerable soul.

These words were written in a hospital bed by William Ernest Henry, a poet who had just endured the amputation of his foot due to tuberculosis of the bone. Henry ends his famous poem, "Invictus," with this:

I am the master of my fate:
I am the captain of my soul.

Here is a sexy idea: "You can do it!" In our society, that message is shouted at us all day long. Everyone from the marketing department at Nike® to Morgan Freeman wants us to believe we can do it on our own. Devastatingly, when it comes to the fate of our souls, we'd all like to think we are unconquerable. We want to think that something we can do will save us. We want to atone for our own sin. We want to focus on what we can do rather than what God has done. We want to circumvent the cross and do religion.

Here's the problem. Our souls are not unconquerable, but rather, we are unrighteous people who will perish in hell unless we are justified. "Justification" is not just a Christian-ese church word. It is a word that is mentioned 48 times in the Bible and a word that means something important. The root of justification is justice. We serve a just God, but we are unjust because of our sin. One day we will stand before God, and in his perfect justice, he will not be able to look upon unjust people and simply declare us just and relieve us of our due penalty. If a human judge did that in a rapist's trial, we would shout in protest. We will have to pay the just penalty for our sin, which is death, unless we can be made just—or in another word, righteous. So the question is this. When you stand before God, what will justify you? What will make you righteous?

Here is what will not make you righteous: your works. Counting on your works to make your righteous before God is called religion. Religion offends God. The prophet Isaiah said in Isaiah 64:6 that our righteous deeds, they are nothing but filthy rags. As gross as it may sound, he was actually referring to filthy rags that are used tampons. I know it's not pretty, but that's what he meant. The Apostle Paul took it one step further in Philippians 3:8 when he said that he counted all of his righteousness as worthless as dung. Yes, poop is in the Bible. Isaiah and Paul used such visually arresting images to make their point: that God finds religion absolutely vile, disgusting, and offensive.

Drawing from Paul's metaphor, I want to illustrate what religion leads to, using something I call the Turd Cycle. This is the inevitable pendulum swing between pride and despair that religion always creates. If you put all of your trust in what you can do, then when you manage to do things right every once in a while, you become prideful and you will sin. On the other hand, when you fail, which is inevitable, you fall into despair and you will sin some more. The problem with religion is twofold: It will not save you, and it will kill you. When you stand before God, if you are holding a steaming pile of dung in one hand and a fistful of tampons in the other, it will not end well. By doing religion, not only are you not making yourself any more righteous, you also are heaping on more disgusting sin.

Here is what will make you righteous: the cross of Jesus Christ. Here's what Paul wrote: *I no longer count on my own righteousness through obeying the law; rather, I become righteous through faith in Christ (Philippians 3:9).* The alternative to religion is grace. In Ephesians 2, Paul wrote that we have been saved by grace. God, being both a just and loving God and a gracious God, sent Jesus to pay the due penalty for our sin on the cross. We are justified by what Jesus did, not by what we do. Our sin must go to the cross. We can't circumvent that with our works.

The cross didn't just take away our sin; it also made us righteous. A lot of us look at the cross as if it just brought our sin score back to zero where it was in Eden and now we are left to become righteous with our own works. That is not true. We are not only freed from the unrighteous life that we lived; we are also credited with the righteous life that Jesus lived. God looks on us and sees the righteousness of Christ. *For he [God] has dressed me with the clothing of salvation and draped me in a robe of righteousness (Isaiah 61:10).*

So you have two options: You can pick up a steaming pile of dung and try to clothe yourself with it, or you can receive God's grace and clothe yourself with the righteousness of Christ. Please believe me when I say that grace is the better option!

Let's look at these two options in the story of the Prodigal Son. You may be very familiar with the story Jesus tells in Luke 15:11-32 about the wealthy man's son who takes his inheritance, runs away, parties until he's broke, and finally hits rock bottom. We have all been prodigal children. The father in the story is God, and we are the son. We have rebelled and run far away from our heavenly father.

I've read this story countless times, but a few weeks ago something new hit me. Something really interesting happens when the son is lying face down in a pig's trough starving to death. He turns to religion. Here's my paraphrase of his internal conversation in verses 17-19: "I know what I can do to get my father to take me back in. I will go back, apologize, and work for him as a hired servant. Even his servants get food to eat, so if I work for him, I'll receive at least some of his favor. Also, if I work hard enough, maybe I can mend my relationship with him."

But an amazing thing happens when the son is on his way home hoping that he will be able to win his father's favor through good works. His dad sees him coming a long way off, sprints up to him, and just smashes him with the gospel. In Luke 15:22-24 the gospel sounds like the ecstatic shouts of an old man: " *'Quick! Bring the finest robe in the house and put it on him. Get a ring for his finger and sandals for his feet. And kill the calf we have been fattening. We must celebrate with a feast, for this son of mine was dead and has now returned to life. He was lost, but now he is found.'"* The son put his trust in his works, but he got hit with grace. When he sees his dad's works (the man throwing a huge party, killing the fatted calf, and clothing him with robes and rings), his own works (the hope that he'd get hired as a janitor) fades into the background. The story makes a happy declaration: *So the party began (Luke 15:24).*

But what if the son had not celebrated? What if he had stuck to his guns, been religious, left the party, and gone to shovel poop in the stables hoping that doing some chores would restore him to his dad? It wouldn't have worked. Not only would he have offended his father again by not participating in the party, but he also would have gotten stuck in the same cycle of self-sufficiency that got him in trouble in the first place: wanting to do it by his own strength and on his own terms. Ironically, he'd be covered in no less poop in the horse stable than he was in the pigsty. Thankfully, that's not how it ends.

So like the lost son who came home, let's forget about what we can do and instead receive our father's grace. Party with your dad. Feast at his table and drink the fine wine. Chug the grace. Enjoy what he has done, and stop relying on what you can do. Because the truth is this: You can't do it, but he already has done it.

What other "sexy ideas" come to mind that our culture, including our church culture, has accepted?

In what ways have you "counted on your works" to make up for bad stuff you've done?

Do the analogies of "poop" and "used tampons" offend you? Why or why not?

Are you offended by yourself as you consider that Christ had to die for you? Why or why not?

How willing have you been or how willing are you to celebrate that God celebrates your return to him, stinking though you may be?

by Kyle Idleman

My middle daughter, Morgan, memorized the Ten Commandments at the age of 8. She wanted to recite them to me, so I lay down next to her on her bed and she began to make her way through the list.

"You shall have no other gods before me," she said. "You shall not make yourselves an idol in the form of anything." On down the list she went, making her father proud as she said each of the commandments.

As she finished, I realized that this was a good opportunity to talk to her about sin. I began to explain to her how the Law and the Ten Commandments essentially allow us to recognize the existence of sin. They reveal to us that we are sinners in need of a Savior. I wanted her to understand this.

I turned to Morgan and said, "Honey, have you ever broken one of these Ten Commandments?" She gave me a shy smile, reluctant to answer. I kept probing. "Morgan, I have told some lies before. Have you ever told a lie?" She nodded. "Have you ever not honored your mom and dad?" She stared at me silently. We both understood this was more of a rhetorical question. We continued making our way through the list. "Morgan, have you ever stolen anything? Have you ever been jealous of what someone else had?"

She could see that this was not going well for her; she was ready to put this trial to a stop.

"Dad, I know one commandment I have never broken," she said. "I have never made for myself an idol in the form of anything."

I resisted the temptation to explain to her that this is the one commandment that all of us have broken more than any of the others. I chose not to quote to her the words of Martin Luther, who pointed out that a person cannot break any of the other commandments without first breaking this one. Instead I smiled and kissed her goodnight, deciding to save this conversation for another time.

As I walked down the steps from her room, I began to wonder how many Christians make the same assumption that my 8-year-old daughter had made. How many read through the Ten Commandments like a checklist, breathing a sigh of relief once they arrive at the one about idols? They run through their logic, thinking, "At least we don't have to worry about this one. After all, we don't worship images of stone or of wood. That was a primitive culture, right? We don't worship idols in our modern-day civilization." This logic, however, could not be more inaccurate.

The Bible contains more than 1,000 references to idolatry, but we like to skip over them as if they do not apply to us. Idolatry, however, is the issue that most of us struggle with. It is the one thing keeping us from living the life God really wants us to live. The truth is, there are gods at war within us, battling for who will sit on the throne of our hearts.

At the age of 110, Joshua stood in front of the nation of Israel to give what he assumed would be his final address. Here is a portion of what he said:

"So fear the Lord and serve him wholeheartedly. Put away forever the idols your ancestors worshiped when they lived beyond the Euphrates River and in Egypt. Serve the Lord alone. But if you refuse to serve the Lord, then choose today whom you will serve. Would you prefer the gods your ancestors served beyond the Euphrates? Or will it be the gods of the Amorites in whose land you now live? But as for me and my family, we will serve the Lord" (Joshua 24:14-15).

Joshua basically presents four choices to his people: They could worship the gods of their ancestors from Mesopotamia; they could worship the gods of the Egyptians, who held them in slavery for 400 years; they could worship the gods of the people in whose land they were now living; or they could worship Yahweh—the one true God. There is not a fifth option. Joshua doesn't say, "Another choice would be that you don't worship anything at all." No, Joshua knew that we are all worshippers of something. We will all choose to worship something, even if it displaces our worship toward the one true God.

Here are a few examples that I have encountered of what idolatry looks like today. A woman is caught cheating on her income taxes and faces a number of criminal charges. Yet she does not even need the money—she is a millionaire many times over. She doesn't even understand why she did it. You ask, "Why did she make this choice?" It is because of idolatry. She worships money, status, and possessions, and her actions have given her away.

Then there is the young man that pulls me over to the side after church and for the first time confesses that he has an addiction to pornography. He explains the downward spiral that started when he first saw images at the age of 13. Now he spends countless hours and thousands of dollars in an effort to fulfill this desire.

However, his confession goes south as he tries to justify his addiction by saying, "I am following Jesus in every other area. It's just this one issue." What he has failed to understand is that this is the issue. There is a battle inside for who is really God in his life. He is making a choice: "Will I worship God, or will I worship sex—a physical feeling? Will I worship the Creator, or will I worship the body he created?" His actions reveal that in this battle, God the Creator is being flicked off the throne of his heart nearly every day so he can look at pictures of people without their clothes on. He will continue to struggle with this until he understands that this is idolatry. Until he replaces the false god with the true God, he will not find victory.

I remember talking to a young man on the phone getting ready to move in with his girlfriend. She is not a Christian; he is.

"God understands," he said. "He knows that I am going to marry her. It's not that big of a deal."

I tried to explain to him that it is a big deal, and it's not just because he is "breaking the rules." He has chosen to worship his relationship with her instead of his relationship with Yahweh. It is an issue of idolatry.

This is a life-changing truth, and I believe that for many people—in their sin struggles—this is the truth that has the potential to set free them. You have tried to beat it; you don't like who you are. However, until God alone sits on the throne of your heart, you will continue to struggle. This is the message from the Bible—a truth that many have chosen to ignore. Everybody worships a god of some kind. If you choose not to worship the one true God, then you by default will worship a surrogate god. Ultimately, worshipping any god other than the one true God is like building a bridge to nowhere.

As you enter into a new season of life, now is the time to identify some of the gods that are at war within you. Let me ask you some questions to help you identify if you are putting your hope and faith in a false god.

The first question to ask: "What am I disappointed with?" Are you disappointed with your financial status, your career, or maybe the home you live in? Are you constantly disappointed with whoever it is you're dating? Whenever we experience ongoing and overwhelming disappointment, it reveals that something in our lives is more important to us than it should be. Asking this question can often reveal something that has become too important to us.

Another question to ask yourself: "How do I spend my money?" What does your checkbook say you worship? The Bible puts it this way: "Where your money is, there your heart will be also." Sometimes I visit churches where the pastor essentially gets up and apologizes for taking up an offering. But really, it is the most tangible act of worship that we have in the service. We say, "God, I have money that is of value to me. I'd like to do selfish things with it, but instead I will give it to you because you are what matters most."

Also ask yourself, "What do I worry about?" Maybe it is losing a job. Maybe you fear that you are not going to be liked by other people, that other people won't be impressed by you. Or perhaps you worry a great deal about getting into the right school or landing the right job when you graduate. Why is that? Oftentimes our worry reveals that something has become too important to us.

Another revealing question is this: "When I am hurt, where do I go for comfort?" When you are stressed out by your classes or your job, do you go out and drink the evening away to deal with the pain you feel? When you are rejected by someone of the opposite sex, do you find comfort by going to the pornographic website you were never going to visit again? Where people turn when they need to be comforted often reveals the false god that is on the throne of their heart. It may be food or shopping. It may even be a friend or a family member. But instead of running to God for help, we turn to an idol.

Finally, ask the question, "What brings me the most joy?" Sure, there are many things that God gives because he wants us to experience joy. However, these gifts should point us back to God and cause us to find increased joy in him. Sometimes the idols in our lives are good things, but when good things become god things, it is idolatry.

So how do we keep the one true God on the throne of our hearts? Open your Bible and take a closer look at Joshua 24. This chapter reveals a few practices that can help us truly make God the Lord of our lives. The first thing is that Joshua reminds his listeners to appreciate what God has done for them. In verses 2-13, he repeats great things that God has accomplished for his people, hoping that they would respond with hearts willing to worship. Likewise, as we remember what God has done for us, it restores him to the position of glory in our lives. We need to regularly celebrate who God is and what he has done for us, and as we do that, he will become what is most important.

The next thing Joshua does is challenge the people to recognize who God is. Verse 19 speaks of God as being holy and jealous. So many of the worship songs we sing focus on who God is, because as we are reminded of his majesty and greatness we can't help but worship. In fact, here's one way that we might define worship: Worship is our response to God for who he is and what he has done for us.

The third thing Joshua does is challenge the people to smash all other gods. *"All right then," Joshua said, "destroy the idols among you, and turn your hearts to the Lord, the God of Israel" (Joshua 24:23).* He calls the people to complete surrender. Now is a great time in your life to smash some other gods. Maybe that means you throw out some DVDs, end an unhealthy relationship, or stop spending your money on something that clearly matters to you more than God matters.

There are gods at war within each of us. They battle for the place of glory in our lives. Much is at stake. For whichever god—or God—is victorious wins control and power over us. And ultimately our god—or God—determines our destinies.

Which of the Ten Commandments have you broken most throughout your life?

In what ways have you not worshipped idols?

How would you have answered Joshua's challenge to the people?

Where is God in your life? Is God the center, or is God just incorporated into it, along with all your other stuff?

What do your answers to the questions given throughout the chapter tell you about your own personal idols?

by Steve Carter

A few years ago, Dave Chappelle up and left the set where he was in the process of filming the third season of his critically acclaimed TV show, *Chappelle's Show*. Dave literally walked out mid-joke. He walked outside the studio, flagged down his driver, got into the car, and went straight to the airport, where he boarded a plane headed directly to South Africa. The crew waited for him to come back, but he never returned.

For days people wondered where he was. Comedy Central executives, his friends, the production crew, and his own wife—the dude didn't tell any of them. He just got on a plane and escaped.

Do you ever wonder why people do the things they do?

In the Scriptures, there was a man by the name of Jacob, and on the eve of preparing to reunite with his estranged brother, Esau, he found himself alone until a man came and wrestled him until daybreak.

Until daybreak?

When the man saw that he would not win the match, he touched Jacob's hip and wrenched it out of its socket. Then the man said, "Let me go, for the dawn is breaking!" But Jacob said, "I will not let you go unless you bless me." "What is your name?" the man asked (Genesis 32:25-27).

This question had haunted Jacob for his entire life. When he was born, the Scriptures say, he came out grasping the heel of his older twin brother, Esau. Jacob wasn't just holding onto the heel; he was clutching the heel with one hand—this little one was trying to pull himself forward so that he could be the older brother. As his parents saw this unfolding, they decided to give him the name Jacob, which means, "He grasps the heel," a euphemism for "deceiver." So

Jacob's parents gave him a name that literally means, "he deceives." As you follow Jacob's life, you begin to see that indeed he was a deceiver.

As Jacob and Esau's father, Isaac, is preparing to die, he calls in the older brother, Esau, to give him a blessing. The blessing was a sacred moment between the father and the firstborn. It was an opportunity to speak prophetically, to call out the divine from within the child, and to remind him of the greater story God was calling him into.

One day when Isaac was old and turning blind, he called for Esau, his older son, and said, "My son." "Yes, Father?" Esau replied. "I am an old man now," Isaac said, "and I don't know when I may die. Take your bow and a quiver full of arrows, and go out into the open country to hunt some wild game for me. Prepare my favorite dish, and bring it here for me to eat. Then I will pronounce the blessing that belongs to you, my firstborn son, before I die" (Genesis 27:1-4).

As this conversation is taking place, the boys' mother, Rebekah, hears everything her husband has said. As Esau grabs his weapons to go hunting, Rebekah quickly runs to Jacob, the younger son and her favorite, and tells him everything she has heard. She then says, *"Now, my son, listen to me. Do exactly as I tell you. Go out to the flocks, and bring me two fine young goats. I'll use them to prepare your father's favorite dish. Then take the food to your father so he can eat it and bless you before he dies"* (Genesis 27:8-10).

Rebekah wants Jacob to be Esau. She tells Jacob to deceive his father so that he may get the blessing. She goes to great lengths to make this happen by preparing the food, picking out an outfit from Esau's closet, and then even taking goatskins and placing them on Jacob's hands and neck so that Isaac will be convinced that Jacob actually is Esau.

Jacob, with dinner prepared and goatskins freshly applied, enters the room to get the blessing.

So Jacob took the food to his father. "My father?" he said. "Yes, my son," Isaac answered. "Who are you—Esau or Jacob?" Jacob replied, "It's Esau, your firstborn son. I've done as you told me. Here is the wild game. Now sit up and eat it so you can give me your blessing." Isaac asked, "How did you find it so quickly, my son?" "The Lord your God put it in my path!" Jacob replied. Then Isaac said to Jacob, "Come closer so I can touch you and make sure that you really are Esau." So Jacob went closer to his father, and Isaac touched him. "The voice is Jacob's, but the hands are Esau's," Isaac said. But he did not recognize Jacob, because Jacob's hands felt hairy just like Esau's. So Isaac prepared to bless Jacob. "But are you really my son Esau?" he asked. "Yes, I am," Jacob replied (Genesis 27:18-24).

The plan works, and the father is tricked into giving an amazing blessing to Jacob. When Esau returns from his hunting excursion and finds that Jacob has deceived him again by stealing his blessing, he says, *"I will soon be mourning my father's death. Then I will kill my brother, Jacob"* *(Genesis 27:41).*

When Jacob hears this, he flees. Then, on that fateful night years later, he finds himself wrestling with a man at the Jabbok River until daybreak. The man asks Jacob, "What is your name?" Up until this moment, Jacob's life has been one giant identity crisis.

A few years ago, I'm in a Chicago hotel room waiting for my friend Joe to finish getting ready, and I'm flipping through channels when I come across Dave Chappelle on Oprah. I had never seen *The Oprah Winfrey Show* before, but obviously she knows what she's doing. At one point she looks at Chappelle and asks, "Why did you do it? Why did you leave for South Africa and not tell anyone? Dave, why did you do it?"

The studio audience is dead silent.

Chappelle begins to cry, makes a quick joke, and then utters these beautifully powerful words: "Because success can take you places that character cannot sustain you." After hearing that, I sat in my hotel room speechless. It all began to make sense—why Chappelle could up and leave the set. It's as if he found himself onstage wrestling with a man within who kept asking him, "What is your name?"

When Jacob is asked this question, he proclaims out loud that his name is Jacob. It is a moment of redemption but a moment that is short-lived because the man quickly responds with these words: *"Your name will no longer be Jacob," the man told him. "From now on you will be called Israel, because you have fought with God and with men and have won"* (Genesis 32:28).

What would you say if someone were to ask you right now, "What is your name?" Would it be the name of some person you're striving to imitate or become, or some phrase someone said once that you're trying to prove—or prove wrong? What is truly leading you?

Our lives can easily be attempts at grasping, clinging, and trying to be people we were never created to be. If those raw places go untouched, they will leak out and begin to lead and direct us. It's in these places we find ourselves trying to lead lives that deceive people around us, our Creator, and ultimately ourselves. My life has been filled with these moments. Moments when I've strived to be someone God never created me to be, moments when I've tried to perform or win the approval of others, moments when my own brokenness was leading the way—and I actually hurt those that I care about most.

I'm learning that it is our responsibility to have the courage to ransack our souls for those raw places that are fractured and to invite our Father to remind us who we were truly created to be. It's comforting to know that this man from the wrestling story in Genesis 32 (who is actually God) gives Jacob a name that means "to struggle"—a name that is drenched in the tension and brokenness of humanity. This name serves as an invitation for us to do the hard work of knowing the person God created us uniquely to be and letting that true identity lead the way.

Have you ever felt like just leaving your life behind and starting over someplace else?

What does your name mean? Does it describe you at all?

In what ways do you feel like your parents led you in the wrong way, like Jacob's mom did to him?

Can you think of a time when God wanted one thing for you but people wanted something else? What was going on? What happened?

Are you willing to let God change your name? If so, what might you hope it would be?

Decisions Made Now Affect Your Future

Dangerous Obedience

As Christians, we have a calling on our lives to listen and follow the Holy Spirit. But even though we know this, we often don't know what this looks like or how to live as people who follow the Spirit's leading with courage. The good news is that Jesus modeled this way of living to us. In the Gospel of Luke, it's mentioned over and over again that Jesus was "led by the Spirit" as he went places.

His followers understood this, too. They saw conversations and miracles and glimpses of God through one man listening to the Spirit. They believed that one act of obedience from one man could change everything— even when the calling was strange or irrational, like going and waiting on the side of the road.

In Acts 8:26, an angel instructed Philip: *"Go south down the desert road that runs from Jerusalem to Gaza."* Philip had already chosen a tough place to minister: Samaria.

But now, to have an angel show up and ask him to go to an unknown location for an unknown project?

Sounds dangerous. Or impulsive. Or illogical. Really, any excuse to get us out of going.

But Philip went. He knew that God's call to advance the kingdom started by following the Spirit, so he was obedient. We often forget that God's call usually requires us to be stretched. That's because we look at our lives through our lens and rarely God's. We don't see how God sees people and the world around us. We see what affects us, what makes us comfortable, and what we want for ourselves.

When Philip started out on his journey, he met an Ethiopian eunuch who had walked into the temple in Jerusalem with questions about understanding the Scriptures and left feeling disappointed and sensing that he didn't belong. Of course, Philip didn't know any of this. He just knew the Spirit was calling him to approach the eunuch's chariot and start a conversation with him.

It helps to understand what the eunuch's life would have been like at that time. He held an important position in the royal court of the queen of Ethiopia and was most likely wealthy. He was without a family since he had been castrated; some cultures believed that men would focus more on their jobs at hand if they didn't have other distractions (I've worked with high school guys, and this is actually pretty accurate). But it was obvious that his wealth and status did not satisfy him.

You get a glimpse of the eunuch's loneliness and hunger for truth in the text. You can sense that the weight of his decisions and confusion had been with him throughout his whole journey, as he returned home with no clearer answers than he had left with. And then Philip approaches him:

Philip ran over and heard the man reading from the prophet Isaiah. Philip asked, "Do you understand what you are reading?" The man replied, "How can I, unless someone instructs me?" And he urged Philip to come up into the carriage and sit with him. The passage of Scripture he had been reading was this: "He was led like a sheep to the slaughter. And as a lamb is silent before the shearers, he did not open his mouth. He was humiliated and received no justice. Who can speak of his descendants? For his life was taken from the earth." The eunuch asked Philip, "Tell me, was the prophet talking about himself or someone else?" So beginning with this same Scripture, Philip told him the Good News about Jesus. As they rode along, they came to some water, and the eunuch said, "Look! There's some water! Why can't I be baptized?" He ordered the carriage to stop, and they went down into the water, and Philip baptized him (Acts 8:30-38).

How amazing is God's timing? He places Philip on a road to meet a man with influence and power who is searching for truth. Not only that, but the man is reading a passage from Isaiah that eventually goes on to tell of how there is a place for everyone because of Christ.

Look at how these words would have brought hope to the eunuch:

"Don't let foreigners who commit themselves to the Lord say, 'The Lord will never let me be part of his people.' And don't let the eunuchs say, 'I'm a dried-up tree with no children and no future.' For this is what the Lord says: I will bless those eunuchs who keep my Sabbath days holy and who choose to do what pleases me and commit their lives to me. I will give them—within the walls of my house—a memorial and a name far greater than sons and daughters could give. For the name I give them is an everlasting one. It will never disappear!" (Isaiah 56:3-5).

In that moment with Philip, a man who had been rejected discovered that he had been included in the gospel message. We're reminded of this over and over again in the Scriptures: that the good news of Jesus is for everyone! This is what compelled Philip—and this is what we must believe if we are to be sent by the Spirit.

Historians say that this eunuch traveled back to Ethiopia and introduced Christianity to his family and eventually his country; 2,000 years later,

Ethiopia stands as a Christian nation among countries dominated by Islam. And just this past year, my wife and I traveled to Ethiopia to pick up our daughter and unite her with our family. Who knows if that even would have been possible if Phillip hadn't followed an irrational call to stand by the road and wait for a chariot?

We never know what God is going to do through one person who is totally committed to him. We never know where one simple act of obeying and following the Spirit might lead. We never know what would change for generations ahead of us if we would simply learn to listen, recognize, and follow the voice of the Spirit.

The following pages focus on how your decisions now can affect your future forever. Be praying as you read that God's voice and leading would be clear and strong in your life and that you would learn every day how to follow where the Spirit leads, however crazy that may be!

by Dave Ferguson

Which would you prefer: receiving a penny today and having it double every day for a month, or receiving $3 million right now? Believe it or not, if I gave you a penny today, and doubled it every day, at the end of 30 days you'd have $5,368,709.12! Imagine if it was a 31-day month!

I don't know about you, but I believe Jesus was being totally serious when he said to his followers, "Go and make disciples of all people." And I take him seriously on that because I believe God is a God of transformation. He's the God of what theologians call the "Missio Dei," Latin for "God with a mission." The mission of God is to transform the world back into what it was originally created to be: God's good, beloved creation, a fully connected community with God as the center and sustainer. And God transforms the world in this really odd way: through people.

So here's where the whole penny thing is important: If we are going to transform the world, we need to not only be transformed ourselves, we also need to be transforming others—and we need to be transforming others into people who then transform others. We need to have the penny thing working for us: One transformed person becomes two, and two become four, which down the line can become millions of people!

I can't take credit for this brilliant exponential strategy—Jesus knew it and lived it. First thing Jesus did when he began his work was to gather a group of people: *"Come, follow me, and I will show you how to fish for people!" (Matthew 4:19).* Jesus got 12 ordinary guys together, shared with them his message and ministry, and then sent them out to invest in others in the same way. Despite all the power and charisma and authority he possessed, Jesus still focused most of his life on transforming others who would transform others. So how did Jesus manage to pull this off? I'm glad you asked!

After Jesus called the first followers together, the Bible makes this seemingly mundane observation: *Then Jesus and his disciples left Jerusalem and went into the Judean countryside. Jesus spent some time with them there, baptizing people (John 3:22).* Jesus spent some time with his disciples, which in Greek translates to "diatreebo," or "to rub against." It became a euphemism for spending time, and it literally means "time spent together rubbing up against each other." So when it says Jesus spent time with his disciples, it was diatreebo—some of him was rubbing off on them. One of the main ways Jesus transformed his followers into people who would transform others who would transform the world was simply to spend time with them.

Here's why this matters so much. When most of us hear this idea that we all need to be people who transform others into people who transform the world, I imagine a pretty sizable number of us think, "I do what I can to help people in need, but I could never transform anybody else. I'm not a spiritual giant, I don't know the Bible very well, I don't pray much. I do what I can, but I don't think I could ever transform anybody." No matter who you are or where you are spiritually, God has put things in you that are meant to change the world. God has placed skills and gifts and abilities and passions and interests and capacities in you that he can use to transform the planet, and if you just spend time with people, what God has put in you and how God has transformed your life can rub off on them.

A good friend of mine had this happen in his own life. A guy joined his small group, and they became friends and started hanging out. This guy always said, "I'm not that spiritual. I don't know the Bible, I don't pray much, I cuss a lot; I'm not a good Christian. I'm not even a very good person." He was serious—but God had put something in him. This guy had a special place in his heart for children who don't have any father figures. Every week he was giving of himself by mentoring two financially under-resourced boys who didn't have dads in their lives. He included these two guys in stuff his family did, and he did stuff with these two guys one on one. (And he already had three kids of his own!) Because my friend was hanging out with him, my friend started thinking, "Maybe I should do that, too?" So he started mentoring a boy who didn't have a dad in his life. And you know what that was? Diatreebo. This "not very spiritual guy" was transforming me.

Have you seen the hit movie *The Blind Side*? Sandra Bullock portrays a woman whose family takes in a teenager in need, and a friend of hers says to her, "You're changing that boy's life." And she responds, "No, he's changing mine." Diatreebo.

Now for the second way Jesus transformed others, and it's something I'll be sold on for the rest of my life. When Jesus transformed his first followers into leaders, in church-language they usually call that "discipleship," but there's a much better word for it: apprenticeship. If you've ever seen the TV show *The Apprentice*, you know what Donald Trump is trying to do: He is looking for someone to train to do what he does, which is basically world financial domination. He's looking for someone to apprentice.

Ram Charan is a leading thinker in business management circles, and he says this: "Apprenticeship is at the heart of the new approach to leadership development. To understand why, you'll have to come to grips with a potentially controversial belief: leadership can only be developed through practice in the real world and converting that experience into improved skill and judgment. That conversion does not take place in the classroom."

Those words come from a very recent book, but a long, long time ago, Jesus knew the value of apprenticeship, and he was doing it. We think of Jesus and the amazing things he did for people in need, but the bulk of this time was spent transforming people through apprenticeship to do the same. And his followers followed suit. The Apostle Paul, for example, did more than just influence people himself. His first apprentice was a guy named Silas. When Paul went out to start churches, he took Silas with him as an apprentice. Then Silas went out to do the same and took another guy along as his apprentice, a guy named John Mark. And Paul started apprenticing another guy, named Timothy. One penny becomes two, and each of those two pennies doubles and so on and so forth, and historians tell us that within the first three centuries, Christ followers grew to well over 50 percent of the population of the Roman Empire. Now that's some serious exponential transformation!

We need every single Christ-follower to be on mission, but we also need every person on this mission to be apprenticing somebody else to be on mission, too. Paul got it—check out what he said to one of his apprentices: *Timothy, my dear son, be strong through the grace that God gives you in Christ Jesus. You have heard me teach things that have been confirmed by many reliable witnesses. Now teach these truths to other trustworthy people who will be able to pass them on to others (2 Timothy 2:1-2).* See the pennies multiplying? That's four generations of apprenticeship: Paul, Timothy, "trustworthy people," "others."

Let me close by telling you what's in it for you. One time a sociologist asked 50 people who were at least 95 years old, "If you could do it all over again, what would you do different?" Three main responses came back: "If I had it to do all over again, I would reflect more, risk more, and do more that will live on after I'm gone."

This is an effective, biblical way to do something that will live on long after you're gone. If you apprenticed one person this year, and at the end of the year, each of you took on a new apprentice, at the end of two years you'd have four leaders. And if you all did it again, at the end of three years you would have eight. After 10 years you'd have—ready for this—1,024 people. After 20 years you'd have 524,288, and at the end of 30 years you'd have 536,870,912 difference-makers. That's way better than $5 million in pennies! And it all starts when one person says, "I'm not only going to be about transforming the world, I'm also going to inspire and encourage others to be difference-makers." And that is something that will live on and on long after you're gone. I don't know about you, but I don't want to just live a satisfying life. I want to do more things that live on after I'm gone, and I believe there's nothing better for that than being a person who seeks to be part of God's process of transforming others!

five questions

What has been your idea of how God transforms the world?

Have you had the perspective of "rubbing off on others" as the way toward transformation? If not, what's your perspective?

What gifts, skills, abilities, and passions has God given you for changing the world?

Who is someone in your life who has "rubbed off" on you, helping to make you more like Christ?

Can you think of someone who you can start influencing intentionally for God's kingdom? How can you start today?

CHAPTER 16

Where Are Paul and Obi-Wan Kenobi?
The Importance of Finding a Mentor

by Aaron Stern

I recently heard a stat that said people who come from churches of 100 people or smaller are more likely to stay engaged in their faith through college. The reason? They know how to interact with people of all ages. When we interact with generations older than us, we learn and glean from their wisdom.

Timothy had Paul. Timothy was a young leader, and Paul was a man of God looking to invest in someone who could succeed him in planting, leading, and pastoring churches. After his heart-transforming, sight-stealing life takeover on the Damascus road, he had years of intense learning in the desert under his belt, and he lived through shipwrecks, beatings, and imprisonment. Paul was a spiritual giant and had a vast amount of life experience to draw from. He wrote 1 and 2 Timothy to his young friend, passing on a lifetime of growth. Timothy looked to Paul for training and advice on how he should lead in the kingdom.

We all need a Paul. Someone with an eye for how we should develop and grow. Someone to provide wisdom and navigational advice about the twists and turns that lie ahead. Someone to encourage, challenge, and direct. Sounds pretty great, doesn't it?

Now before you run off and try to find Paul, let me tell you about Tom. He's 66 years old, and we meet for coffee or lunch once every month or two. Tom is no Paul (sorry, Tom). He hasn't written half the New Testament or been imprisoned for his faith, but he has incredible life experience and is definitely a wise man. I haven't always met with Tom. It wasn't until a few years ago that I started being intentional about making time for men like Tom. You see, I was looking for someone who didn't exist. I was looking for the Apostle Paul—or at least a close relative of his. Just like Luke Skywalker had Obi-Wan Kenobi, I wanted a mentor who had it all: the guy who could speak into every area of my life, could see my future, and could prepare me for all things.

Even though I had this idealistic picture in my head of the perfect mentor-sage, I wasn't looking very hard for him. I thought that if it was important for me, then it would just happen and this mentor would just land in my life. My lack of trying came from little effort and mostly from the belief that I didn't think I needed anyone. I am a pretty confident guy, and I had bought into the lie of our culture that says that need is weakness, and independence and individuality are signs of strength. But to take a look at the Scriptures, you don't have to dig very deep to find that wisdom is something that we should pursue with an incredible amount of fervor and intentionality (Proverbs 3:13-18) and that God designed us to need the strength of others (Romans 12:4-5, Ecclesiastes 4:9-12). The easy conclusion is that finding a Paul, an Obi-Wan, or a Tom is a pretty big priority.

Proverbs 13:20 gives a hint for gaining wisdom when it says, *Walk with the wise and become wise.* So just like Timothy walked with Paul and I am walking with Tom, you need to walk with people who are wiser than you.

One of the questions I hear most often as a college pastor is, "I need an mentor; can you find one for me?" I am a proponent of mentorship, but I am not a big fan of formal mentoring programs for college students, so instead of taking their name and number and connecting them with an older person just waiting to be a mentor, I prefer to give a few helpful tips for it to develop more organically.

Don't look for one mentor; look for a team of mentors. I meet with Tom, but I also periodically meet with Paul and with Garvin. The chances of finding one person who embodies everything you hope to be and do are slim to none, so look for different people who display various aspects of life that you admire: the way they raise their children, how they interact with their spouse, they way they deal with disappointment, how they carry themselves, the way they balance life and work, how they manage their money, and so on. By being diverse in whose advice you seek, you will disperse the weight of responsibility and pressure.

Don't ask them to be your mentor. I know several people who have told me that they feel intimidated and overwhelmed by the question "Will you be my mentor?" Regardless of whether that is because they question if they have what it takes, have a preconceived idea of a huge time commitment, or had a poor mentoring experience themselves, you can use a better approach. When you find someone who you would like to learn from or someone that you admire, say something like this: "I have noticed the way you raise your family/run your business/do ministry and would love to learn from you. Would you mind if I bought you a cup of coffee and asked you some questions sometime?" I have never met anyone that isn't completely honored by that request and feels confident in responding to some questions and talking about their lives.

Don't ask for time commitment. You may get together for coffee just once, or maybe this becomes a recurring meeting and developing relationship. Asking to meet without assuming more than one meeting eliminates pressure and allows the relationship to develop naturally without forcing something that isn't a good fit.

Prepare lots of questions. When you meet for coffee (offer to pay for theirs, too), you should have more questions ready than you have time to ask. Again, take the pressure off them. Let them just show up. You asked to meet, so don't just sit there and expect them to have laser vision into what is going on in your life. I always bring a notebook with me when I meet with a mentor, and I usually take notes, depending on the environment. I believe it signifies honor and communicates that I value their time. Here are a few questions that may help you get you started:

- What do you know now that you wish you knew at my age?

- How did you begin your friendship with Jesus, and what has your journey with him been like?

- What do you think has helped you grow in God?

- How have you navigated disappointment in life?

- What are some things that you have done to succeed in _____?

Don't overlook your parents (or grandparents). Sometimes we are looking to the horizon when the best mentors are right in front of our faces. You can grow up thinking that these family members aren't cool or don't know what's up, but step back and take a closer look. Your parents know you better than anyone else and may actually be perfect people to provide input and advice.

It is never too early to start, and spending time with older people is never wasted time.

five questions

Have you ever thought about the opportunity of having a mentor? Are you willing to be mentored?

Have you had someone who mentored you? What were the distinctive things about this person?

What kind of mentor do you think would help you most in your life right now?

What questions would you ask a mentor-type person if you could? Take some time to write down some of those questions.

Are you willing to ask God to connect you with someone who would be a blessing to you as a mentor? Why not do that right now?

by Kyle Idleman

A waiting room can be a pretty good illustration of our lives. We spend our days waiting in lines; we sit in our cars waiting for red lights to turn green. We wait, but we do not always do it well. When waiting, we often grow frustrated and all we can think about is getting whatever it is we are waiting for so we don't have to wait any longer. But almost immediately we find ourselves waiting on something else. Truly, much of life involves waiting.

Oftentimes we would have to define our waiting as waiting on God for something. We are waiting for God to land us a job, to heal us of sickness, to bring along someone we can spend the rest of life with. The list goes on and on. Is this where you are—waiting on God to move? Do you ever feel like you are sitting in God's waiting room while everyone's name is called but your own? You sit and you wait.

As we study in Scripture what happens in God's waiting room, we see something surprising: What God does in us while we are waiting is often more important than whatever it is we are waiting for. The Bible is full of teachable examples where individuals sat in God's waiting room and were better off because of it.

One example comes from the life of David. The story begins in 1 Samuel 16 when David was just a young man—about 12 years old. A special guest, the prophet Samuel, had come to visit his home. David, however, was left by his older brothers to tend the sheep. Samuel has David called in from the fields and he anoints him with oil. We don't know if Samuel told David that day the purpose of this anointing—to be the next king of Israel—but it happened right in front of his brothers.

But after this event, for the most part, things just went back to normal for David. God says, "Go back to herding sheep. I'll let you know when the time has come." As time passed, David gained prominence—killing a giant will do that—but his life grew burdensome as he began to face difficult situations because of his position as future king: narrowly escaping attempts on his life and fleeing through the wilderness. It would be many years and many hardships before David would finally step into the position he had been promised early on in his life.

Here's my question: Why didn't God wait to make such a promise until, say, a month before it was time for David to become king? Wouldn't that have been easier on David? Why anoint him so early, leaving him to wait years for this promise to be fulfilled? It seems that God didn't plan this out very well. All that waiting seems so unnecessary.

In reality, however, there is a vital purpose for David's waiting. During that time he learned significant lessons that led him to become a God-honoring man. He went through those experiences knowing that they would assist him once he became king. The same is true for all of us. God is often more concerned about who we become during a season of waiting than whatever it is that we are waiting to see happen. Think of it this way: Waiting is an essential part of becoming.

During this process, David chose to wait actively. We see this exemplified when Goliath threatened the armies of Israel. Embracing his faith in God, David faced and defeated the giant with a sling and some stones. He did not stay stagnant; he actively engaged with the situation that was presented to him, serving God faithfully.

We, too, should learn to wait actively. The temptation is to think of waiting as a waste where we sit on our hands just killing time. This is what we do in the doctor's office, right? You sit there and do nothing—at most you flip through a magazine that is 3 years old. You are just killing time until someone calls your name.

We often act the same way when waiting on God. We think that our best option is to passively do nothing while we wait for God to make a move.

This, however, is not the example we see in David's life or elsewhere in Scripture. Instead, we see individuals waiting actively. If you are waiting for God to provide food, you do not just sit on your couch and say, "Man, I'm hungry—I hope God brings me something quick because I could really use something to eat." No, you go into the kitchen and make a sandwich. A similar approach should be used where we, like David, are putting ourselves in a position to glorify God and advance his purposes while waiting on him to keep his promise.

We often have this idea that it is God's job to fulfill the very specific plans that we have. However, that is not waiting on God; that is waiting on whatever it is that we want. Instead, when you're in God's waiting room, choose this mentality: "God, I will serve you while I'm waiting." Whether you are waiting to get married, to get a job, or to decide what your major will be, find ways to serve God actively as you wait.

David also chose to wait patiently. In 1 Samuel 24, King Saul and about 3,000 of his men were searching for David in desert caves. Here's what it says in verse 3: *At the place where the road passes some sheepfolds, Saul went into a cave to relieve himself.* Basically Saul told his men, "You guys wait here. I'm going to step into the men's room." What Saul did not know, however, was that David and his men were hiding in that very same cave! David's men urged him to kill Saul—to take the shortcut, because with one swing of his sword David's problems could end. But David chose otherwise. Instead of cutting the king's throat, David simply cut a corner from Saul's cloak. Then, after Saul had exited the cave, David emerged and spoke, holding up this piece of cloak. *"May the Lord judge between us. Perhaps the Lord will punish you for what you are trying to do to me, but I will never harm you"* (1 Samuel 24:12).

What an incredible response! God had made it clear to his people that no one was to lay a hand on the Lord's anointed, and David was aware of this command. It was not David's job to take out Saul—that was up to God. Through his actions, David teaches us that waiting on God not only means waiting actively, but it also means waiting patiently. David knew that God would take care of things when he wanted to take care of them, and David was not going to force it.

Nevertheless, waiting patiently is hard, especially when God seems slow and his timetable doesn't match up with yours. You are single, longing for intimacy, but there are no good choices around you so you lower your standards and justify your shortcuts. You are seeking a respectable job, but as time goes by, you sacrifice your integrity to make money in a shameful business. We lose patience and take matters into our own hands, as if we could control the situation better than God can. However, God's timing is better than our timing, and God's way is better than our way.

Ultimately, our waiting leads to the result of God fulfilling his promise to us, and we look forward to that fulfillment with great excitement! Even David, who lived many years as a fugitive, looked forward to God's promise with eager expectancy. He knew that God's timing would be perfect and that the result would be great. Take a note from David and learn to wait with a sense of expectancy. This is not a doctor's office waiting room experience that we want to end quickly. No, this is an "I can't wait" response. There is a sense of expectancy; there is a sense of hope. We know that God is going to keep his promise, and we know that God's promises are going to be fulfilled.

God's waiting room is a place where you can grow and learn to trust. God is faithful and has your best interest at heart. So when you feel like God is running late—that his timetable isn't matching up with your master plan—you wait on him. It is in God's waiting room that you will either grow and mature or rebel and wither. If you allow God to do his work, you will find that what God did in you while you were waiting was ultimately more important than whatever it is you were waiting for.

What are some situations that require waiting on any given day? What goes through your mind as you are waiting?

What has been your attitude toward "waiting on God"?

Do you see any ways that God is developing you as you wait on him? What are they?

What things in your life define how you wait on God?

What is your response when you are offered "shortcuts" to God's timing? Do you recognize them? Do you take them? Do you wait more?

by Karl Halverson

There can be nothing but transparency in something like this: I am the product of the sins of my parents. I can't hide from who they were and how it has affected who I am. I was born about 42 years ago. My father had been married to my mother before my birth. At my birth, though, she was single and alone. He chose to leave and, as I came to find out much later in life, marry at least 5 other times. I am the progeny of a womanizing father and a mother who struggled deeply with the sins of the '60s.

With age came knowledge of the effects of my parents' sin on me. I learned that the lusts of my flesh burned with furnace intensity and that relief could be found in acceptable cultural norms of visual stimulation as quenchers of insatiable appetite. I realized that the pride of my life, so aptly pursued in activities that lifted me up and put others down, could make me the god such pride demanded. I learned that satisfying the lust of my eyes with things like clothes and cars and TVs could seemingly bring satisfaction beyond that of a heart transformed. From young boy to young man, I learned that I was the product of the sins of my parents.

It was as a man that I discovered the consequences of such lust and pride. The consequences of the lusts of my flesh limited who I had been created to be and the relationships I had been created to have. The end answer of the query of pride was the humility and humiliation before God and man since I, in fact, was not and never would be a god. The final destination of the lust of my eyes was that all of those things that beckoned to me to own them actually became my masters, and if I didn't break the bonds of their enslavement, I would forever wallow in the muck of materialism as a pig does in the mud and stench of its pen. It is as a grown man that I realized the implications of the sins of my parents. Understanding these implications was essential to getting away from those barbed-wire, quicksand-like entanglements.

That's my story.

What about another story? One of the main characters was a woman dragged to and thrown at the feet of Jesus by legalistic hypocrites. She was clothed only in what she could grab after being torn from the arms of her lover. There she stood, condemned in front of God's own Son. Humiliation marked her face because she knew she'd been "caught in the act." Fear gripped her heart for she knew the punishment for this sin: death. She wasn't the only character, though. I've mentioned the legalist hypocrites who cared about nothing but their own pride. There is also Moses, whose name was invoked as just cause to accuse this woman (and Jesus). Then there's Jesus, who'd been having an enjoyable time instructing his followers on the ways of God in their lives.

The story in John 8 unfolds into a drama of interpersonal conflict, a challenge to the authority of Jesus, and an eye into parental sins reaching their ignored and undesired ends. "This woman is an adulterer," the accusers said. "We caught her having sex with a man who is not her husband," they accuse. "What are you going to do about it, teacher of the law, Rabbi, godly man!?" Jesus' answer was very perplexing because it included none of the intrigue, titillation, and drama for which the accusers had hoped to see. He casually, even flippantly, bent down and wrote words on the ground. They kept on challenging him to tell them what he would do; all he did was write. Then he stood up and through clenched teeth (based on examples of his interaction with hypocrites like this before) challenged them: *"If any one of YOU is without sin, let…him…be the first to throw a stone at her."* Then back to his ground musings.

The hypocrites started walking away, one by one, the older ones first. Finally, it was only Jesus and the woman. She stood there, still barely dressed, still condemned, still humiliated, still fearful. Yet Jesus brought to light the reality and hope of the situation. There was actually no one left to condemn the woman (or Jesus). In fact, Jesus, the righteous Son of God himself, wasn't left to condemn her. He sent her away, but not without a warning, a challenge, and hope. *"I do not condemn you. Go now, and leave your life of sin."* With that, this story ends.

What's the point of sharing this story with you? There could be so many. The richness of the lives could be considered and contemplated for a very long time. My desire, though, is to show how the characters are reflections of their parents' lives. The hypocrites reflect the attitude of oppression and condemnation that was conveyed to them through the lives of their parents. The woman reflects the way she may have been treated by her parents or the way her father had treated other women. We can even see glimpses of their spiritual father Moses, who, although holy through faith in God, had solved his problems with anger and violence, as the Pharisees were doing with the woman. Each of these characters reflects the sins of their parents.

Jesus saw this. He saw the sins of the hypocrites. He saw the sins of the woman. He even remembered the sins of Moses. And Jesus called each one of them to be responsible for their own sins. He didn't, though, leave them responsible to solve the problem of their sin. He showed them his way of solving sin: compassion, mercy, forgiveness, and second chances (and third chances and fourth chances and so on).

He could have (should have?) condemned the hypocrites for their sins. He knew they were sinners and they knew they were sinners, but he didn't condemn them. He could have (should have?) condemned the woman for her sin but he didn't. There was no hiding her sin, as she stood before him in her hastily grabbed garments.

I can't tell you how to solve all of this in your life. In fact, I would be errant if I offered you "five principles of escaping the sins of your parents." All I can do is lay a challenge before you which is simply this: Pursue God and his work in all of history to bring us to himself in rightness and wholeness. The place this pursuit starts and from which it always continues is God's revelation of himself to us, the Bible.

I think that, in one way or another, we can all relate to what I've just written. We can all put our fingers on the struggles we have with how our parents have lived, whether it's the seemingly benign sin of a father who is late home every night because he's helping others or the gross (in its original sense of "huge") sin of parents abandoning their children for the sake of their own pleasures. What may be difficult for us to understand, though, is that we are completely responsible for our own sins, even though they stem from those of our parents.

What this means is that we're not off the hook. We can't say to ourselves or to others, "Well, my parents screwed me up so it's their fault that I'm this way and that I'm doing these things." We must accept that our sins are now our sins, no matter their roots in the lives of our parents. Look at what James says: *"Where do you think all these appalling wars and quarrels come from? Do you think they just happen? Think again. They come about because you want your own way, and fight for it deep inside yourselves. You lust for what you don't have and are willing to kill to get it. You want what isn't yours and will risk violence to get your hands on it" (James 4:1-2 The Message).* When you read the words "wars and quarrels," read "sin." Why do we sin? Because we don't have what we want to have. Why do we do wrong? Because we decide, for ourselves, to try and get what we don't have.

If we are only willing to admit it, we can come to terms with the cause of our sins. We might be tempted to take what I've written up to this point and blame our parents for the entire struggle we have with sin. My oldest son likes to do that. "Dad, you are the one who has shown me how to act like this!" That's not at all fair, though. Why? Well, although it may be our parents who have sinned before us and even inclined us to sin, it is not they who force us to continue on any sort of "sin way."

We are our own keepers of the sin way. We are responsible for our own sin actions. Our parents may have shown us the way, but we keep ourselves on the way. In saying to the woman caught in adultery, "Go and sin no more," Jesus was saying, "Go on your way but don't follow your old ways, the ways your parents taught you and the ways they exampled for you."

What can be done then? As I look at my life and see the twisted mass of failed dreams and plans for God's kingdom and will, I wonder if there is anything that can bring about a transformation of evil to good; wickedness to righteousness; death to life; parental misdirection to personal redirection. If I were to continue in ending everything in myself, then there would be no hope. If I were to continue to look only at what can be seen, then the reality of the eternalness of the unseen would forever be blocked from my view.

So I must look beyond myself; I must look beyond my sight and look to another who is greater than I am and who is the actual eternal way for which I have been searching. I must look for one who has no history of generational sin but whose history is intricately entwined with the sins of the generations as the "Bringer of generational righteousness."

Of course, there is only one who fits this description: It is Jesus Christ. He, as the God-Man, has only a history of purity and righteousness (although tempted in every way, like us, as Hebrews 4 says). He, as the one who takes the sins of the world, is the history of God in the lives of people, entwined as he has been since the foundation of the world to take the sins of the world. He, as the righteousness of God, wipes away the generations of sin and ushers in the generations of righteousness in the lives of those who call on his name by faith. He is the only one who has what is needed to break the passing on of sin from parents to children.

It is but mine to believe that Jesus is this bringer of generational righteousness. It is mine, in the midst of my marriage, to believe that Christ is the righteousness needed to break the lusts of my flesh. It is mine, in the midst of my relationship to my children, to believe that Christ is the righteousness needed to unite me with them as their guide toward him. It is mine, in the midst of pride, to believe only in Christ as the boast of righteousness in my life. It is mine, in the midst of affluence, to relinquish control of my material needs by believing that Christ is the sustenance of my physical life. It is mine only to believe in Christ, and it is his to be everything else.

He is yours like this, too, fellow sons and daughters of sinners. There is no easy formula for what all of this means. There is only a road on which you can walk and on which God is the companion, guide, and destination. All I can tell you is to walk on the way that God has given you by, through, and to himself. All I can tell you is what Jesus said: "Go and sin no more as your parents did."

five questions

In what ways might you be the product of or feel the impact of your parents' sins?

In the story about the woman being brought to Jesus, to which character do you best relate? Why?

In what ways do you pursue God in order to be made holy by him?

How might you be blaming your parents for the sin in your life as an adult?

What are the sins you need to walk away from as you walk toward and with God?

by Mike Hickerson

I learned some important lessons at an early age via Marty McFly, Doc Brown, Biff (every villain should be named Biff), a souped-up DeLorean, and a flux capacitor with 1.21 gigawatts. The *Back to the Future* movie trilogy taught me a lot about life: hoverboards, time travel, the importance of the year 1985, and how the past impacts the future!

Funny thing: Spiritually speaking, I think we all have a past, a present, and a future! All of us have a past—our "was"—and it's the only "was" we are ever going to have. I've been learning that my present—my "is"—sometimes gets held back by what happened to me in my "was" or what I've done in my "was." Even further, my "was" can keep me from leaning into my "is," which hampers my "is to come."

Got it?

I believe what God says in Revelation 1:8 is true: *"I am the Alpha and the Omega—the beginning and the end," says the Lord God. "I am the one who is, who always was, and who is still to come—the Almighty One."*

I'm learning a new formula: Forgiven "was" + Intentional "is" = Full "is to come." But I also am learning that I can't get around this principle: My past impacts my present and my future, for good or bad! My past isn't neutral; I learn from it, grow from it, ignore it, or repeat it.

I always thought that if I just left my past alone, I could go on with life and it wouldn't bother me again. But in my 20s, I started realizing that the stuff in my past that I had swept under the rug had been growing (and in some cases rotting) and was beginning to seep out into my everyday life!

I started looking back—I mean way back—so I could see the best way to move forward. I went back to the Old Testament, and I began to find my answers.

High Places

In the Old Testament, I kept seeing references to "high places" that were set up to worship anything and everything other than the one true God. I also realized that the kings entrusted with leading God's people displayed one of three basic reactions to these "high places."

Some kings allowed their construction:

- *During Rehoboam's reign, the people of Judah did what was evil in the Lord's sight, provoking his anger with their sin, for it was even worse than that of their ancestors. For they also built for themselves pagan shrines and set up sacred pillars and Asherah poles on every high hill and under every green tree (1 Kings 14:22-23).*

- *They had followed the practices of the pagan nations the Lord had driven from the land ahead of them, as well as the practices the kings of Israel had introduced. The people of Israel had also secretly done many things that were not pleasing to the Lord their God. They built pagan shrines for themselves in all their towns, from the smallest outpost to the largest walled city. They set up sacred pillars and Asherah poles at the top of every hill and under every green tree. They offered sacrifices on all the hilltops, just like the nations the Lord had driven from the land ahead of them. So the people of Israel had done many evil things, arousing the Lord's anger. Yes, they worshiped idols, despite the Lord's specific and repeated warnings. Again and again the Lord had sent his prophets and seers to warn both Israel and Judah: "Turn from all your evil ways. Obey my commands and decrees—the entire law that I commanded your ancestors to obey, and that I gave you through my servants the prophets." But the Israelites would not listen. They were as stubborn as their ancestors who had refused to believe in the Lord their God (2 Kings 17:8-14).*

Some kings tolerated their existence:

- *Solomon loved the Lord and followed all the decrees of his father, David, except that Solomon, too, offered sacrifices and burned incense at the local places of worship (1 Kings 3:3).*

- *Although the pagan shrines were not removed, Asa's heart remained completely faithful to the Lord throughout his life (1 Kings 15:14).*

And some kings removed them:

- *He [Hezekiah] did what was pleasing in the Lord's sight, just as his ancestor David had done. He removed the pagan shrines, smashed the sacred pillars, and cut down the Asherah poles. He broke up the bronze serpent that Moses had made, because the people of Israel had been offering sacrifices to it. The bronze serpent was called Nehushtan (2 Kings 18:3-4).*

- *And the king [Josiah] went up to the Temple of the Lord with all the people of Judah and Jerusalem, along with the priests and the prophets—all the people from the least to the greatest. There the king read to them the entire Book of the Covenant that had been found in the Lord's Temple. The king took his place of authority beside the pillar and renewed the covenant in the Lord's presence. He pledged to obey the Lord by keeping all his commands, laws, and decrees with all his heart and soul. In this way, he confirmed all the terms of the covenant that were written in the scroll, and all the people pledged themselves to the covenant. Then the king instructed Hilkiah the high priest and the priests of the second rank and the Temple gatekeepers to remove from the Lord's Temple all the articles that were used to worship Baal, Asherah, and all the powers of the heavens. The king had all these things burned outside Jerusalem on the terraces of the Kidron Valley, and he carried the ashes away to Bethel (2 Kings 23:2-4).*

Part of me wants to laugh at Israel and Judah and say, "Make up your mind"—but then I realize that parts of their stories remind me of my story. I'm reminded of the times that I have built my own "high places" of worship for anything and everything other than God, "high places" like fame, pleasure, acceptance, success, money, power, and winning, just to name a few. I remember times I've been comfortable trying to let those things coexist on the throne of my life with God. I also think about those times I've had the courage to smash the high places in my life.

What about you? Do you have any high places that you've built recently? Do you have any high places that you built years ago but continue to tolerate? Are there any high places that you need to tear down?

As I look back to go forward in my own life, I realize that it's not enough just to do the demolition work on the high places. I have to do the work to remember how faithful God has been and what life he is calling me toward.

It's been helpful for me to look back at the Old Testament again to learn how to go forward in remembering.

Stones of Remembrance
The Old Testament is full of stories of God's people using stones to honor God (check out Genesis 35:14-15; Exodus 24:4; Joshua 24:25-26; 1 Samuel 7:12). They would build these stones of remembrance for a few reasons:

- Remembering how faithful God had been to the person

- Passing on the story of God to the next generation

- Telling the story of God to a watching world

Here's my favorite of these stories:

So Joshua called together the twelve men he had chosen—one from each of the tribes of Israel. He told them, "Go into the middle of the Jordan, in front of the Ark of the Lord your God. Each of you must pick up one stone and carry it out on your shoulder—twelve stones in all, one for each of the twelve tribes of Israel. We will use these stones to build a memorial. In the future your children will ask you, 'What do these stones mean?' Then you can tell them, 'They remind us that the Jordan River stopped flowing when the Ark of the Lord's Covenant went across.' These stones will stand as a memorial among the people of Israel forever." So the men did as Joshua had commanded them. They took twelve stones from the middle of the Jordan River, one for each tribe, just as the Lord had told Joshua. They carried them to the place where they camped for the night and constructed the memorial there. Joshua also set up another pile of twelve stones in the middle of the Jordan, at the place where the priests who carried the Ark of the Covenant were standing. And they are there to this day (Joshua 4:4-9).

I've been learning that I have a hard time remembering: I lose keys, phones, wallets, and all kinds of other things at an alarming rate! I am just a guy who tends to forget. I think God knew that we would be a people that tend to forget. We forget how faithful God has been. We forget how we've been rescued. We forget we are the people of God. We forget to tell God's stories. So to a people that tend to forget, God has us build stones of remembrance to mark those moments along the way of his faithfulness.

What events in your life help you to look back and remember how faithful God has been to you? As we all walk forward, what are some ways you can be intentional about collecting "stones" to help remember his faithfulness to you?

God is constantly using our past to strengthen us, to mold us into the people he wants us to be. Going "back to the future" is a way to reveal how far God has brought us and how perfect his plan is. We need to do the hard work of destroying the "high places" and building the stones of remembrance. While I'm still waiting on my hoverboard from the future, I am remembering the best way to move forward is to go back!

Spiritual Disciplines

God Is an Interrupter

We're all taught as children that interrupting someone is rude. My kids do it when I'm on the phone or after church when I'm talking with someone about something personal. My 6-year-old decides it's time for our family to leave, and as much as I try to train my children to be polite and to not yell "Daddy!" a dozen times when I'm on the phone, they just don't get it. For a child, the needs of now are more pressing than any social expectation that we place on them.

We hate interruptions. We have important things to do and important tasks to accomplish. We have schedules to keep and people to meet and things to create.

But God is an interrupter. God always interrupts. God has done it to me all of my life, ever since I first came to follow him. We even see God interrupt in Scripture since the beginning of time: He interrupted Noah with a request for a boat. Abraham with a call to a distant land. Moses with the request to lead. Joshua with a coat and a dream. Mary, the mother of Jesus, with an angel.

Then when God became flesh and walked on earth, he constantly interrupted people's lives. It didn't matter if you were a fisherman, tax collector, prostitute, or Pharisee. He'd interrupt your profession or rituals for something much more important. And then his death on the cross became an interruption; it can't simply be ignored. It's called generations of people to respond, no matter where they are in life or what they are accomplishing.

Many of us have tried to place God in a box and create our own god, one who rarely, if ever, interrupts our lives, one who enjoys being ignored. There are many in our culture who simply believe God exists to make our lives better, to make our lives safe and comfortable. But in his essence, God is an interrupter.

God has taken many shapes in these interruptions. When I was in junior high, he took the shape of a speaker at a conference who called a generation of teenagers to full-time Christian ministry. Before I knew it I was standing at the altar of the giant auditorium committing my life to ministry. Prior to that, I had big dreams of playing in the NBA®, and if that fell through, I would coach basketball or maybe write for the sports section at the local newspaper. Even at my young age, God was interrupting.

When I was in college, God took the form of a residence hall director who interrupted my beliefs about God and taught me that following God was not simply about rules and regulations. He taught me that God was more than my religion and that my judgmental spirit was one of my greatest sins.

God interrupted me in the form of a small child at an orphanage who latched onto me the moment I arrived and never let go. His was the first diaper I changed, the first little face I cleaned, and he never spoke a word to me because he was much too young for that. But God spoke through him. And many years later God interrupted my life with trips to Africa and a broken heart for children who had no mothers or fathers to look after them. God interrupted my life with the call to adopt and with a baby girl named Claire from Ethiopia.

God has interrupted my life through neighbors. We recently moved to the urban center of Louisville, Kentucky, and the need for mercy is overwhelming. Each time a homeless man knocks on our door asking for help, I know it is God interrupting. Each time a need in our community is discovered but no one else wants to listen, I know it is God interrupting.

God has interrupted my career, my hopes and dreams, and my finances much more often than I would like. He has interrupted me as a father and as a son, as a brother and as a husband, as a friend and as a pastor. In fact, God's interruptions come so frequently that I rarely want to listen to or acknowledge them.

These interruptions reveal our true loves. They reveal what we value most. They reveal the dark places in our hearts that still belong to us, even though we gave our lives to God long ago. They reveal the real me, my greed and selfishness. They reveal my fears and my lack of trust. Most of all, these interruptions simply reveal my sin.

Every great movement of the gospel has come because someone has listened to the interruptions of God. I have a friend whose life was interrupted with a call to spread the gospel, and she gave up a full-ride scholarship to the school of her dreams to serve the poor and the broken in the inner city. I know a family who quit their jobs and left the corporate world because God called them to serve women in the sex industry. Our favorite babysitter is giving up her house, her friends, and her comfort, and moving to Uganda because God interrupted her life on a mission trip to Kenya. I know a college student who sold his car and decided he could catch the bus to school every day because he wanted to give to a new church plant.

I could go on and on, but the real question for us every day is not just will we listen, but will we make our lives available for interruptions?

Hebrews 11 is one of my favorite passages in all of Scripture. It reads like the "Hall of Fame" of the Bible. It simply explains how each member of this great congregation of witnesses was open to God's interruptions, and how they by faith followed where he led:

All these people died still believing what God had promised them. They did not receive what was promised, but they saw it all from a distance and welcomed it. They agreed that they were foreigners and nomads here on earth. Obviously people who say such things are looking forward to a country they can call their own. If they had longed for the country they came from, they could have gone back. But they were looking for a better place, a heavenly homeland. That is why God is not ashamed to be called their God, for he has prepared a city for them (Hebrews 11:13-16).

Too often I imagine that God is following me—waiting to direct me, waiting to tell me what is right, waiting to steer me on the correct path when I wander a bit too far. The problem with that picture is this: I was called to follow God, not the other way around. The interruptions are God's call, and for too long the people of God have failed to listen.

We are comfortable...but not obedient. We are safe...but not secure. We are prosperous...but not satisfied. We are informed...but not aware. We are surrounded...but somehow alone. We are busy...but never quite interrupted.

My prayer for you today is that you are interrupted. I pray that God shatters the illusion of your control. I pray God speaks loudly, inconveniently, and recklessly. I pray that you stop taking him along on your journey, and you begin to let your life be so interrupted that you start to follow him! So speak now, Father; your servants are listening, no matter how busy we are.

The following pages are about specific disciplines we need to develop in order to be used and available to God working around us. I know many of you are away from home for the first time, so as you read, evaluate! Are you open for God's interruptions, and are you available to do the work required of becoming more like God every day?

by Dave Ferguson

A father took his son to McDonald's®, where he proceeded to buy the boy some Super Size® French Fries. While driving back home, the fries smelled so good that the dad reached over and took one little fry out of his son's bag and ate it. The boy got upset and yelled, "Dad you can't have that one. These are *my* fries!"

The dad said he immediately had three thoughts: "First, I thought this kid has forgotten that I am the source of all fries. I brought him here, I took him to McDonald's®, I placed the order, I paid for the order, I handed them to him, and I'm driving him back home. He wouldn't have any fries if it weren't for me. The only reason he got any fries was because of me, the great fry giver!

"Second, I thought about how my kid doesn't realize I could take them away in a second if I wanted to. Or on the other hand I could buy him an entire truckload of fries if I wanted to because I have the power to do either.

"And third, I don't need his fries. I could easily get my own. I could buy myself a hundred orders of them if I wanted to. I just wanted him to learn to be generous!"

Do you think God is like that with us? Maybe God has similar thoughts: "Without me, you would have zip, nothing, nada!" Second, "I could take it away from you just like that, or I could double it just like that, because I've got the power." And finally, "I don't need your fries. I don't need your money. I just want you to learn to be generous."

God just wants us to be generous. And I believe that deep down, we all want to be generous people. So what stops us from being generous? I think we have all sorts of excuses: "I want to be generous, but I just can't afford it right now." "The economy is in such a tough spot right now." "If I only had _____, then I could be really generous."

But despite all this, I am convinced that the biggest factor in whether a person is generous or stingy isn't about how the health of the economy, and it isn't about how much money is in the bank; it's about motivation.

I was thinking about places where I try to be generous: giving money to the church, providing money to the under-resourced, performing spontaneous acts of kindness for strangers, donating time to work in situations that will give people a hand-up, and so on. And as I thought about things I've done intending to be generous and what motivates me, I uncovered a lot of different motivations.

The truth is, sometimes I'm generous because of the reward. I know it's not very noble, but truthfully, sometimes I give to make myself look good or make others think better of me. Or I do it in hopes of a blessing or a "thank you" or appreciation. The Bible is clear that there are rewards for generosity: *Whoever sows sparingly will also reap sparingly, and whoever sows generously will also reap generously (2 Corinthians 9:6 NIV).* God even says when it comes to generosity, *"I will pour out a blessing so great you won't have enough room to take it in! Try it! Put me to the test!" (Malachi 3:10).* And I have experienced the rewards of generosity. But should the rewards be my motivation?

Sometimes I give hoping that my generosity might change something. I'm giving for results! I often give to help someone (like a child) have a better life and do my part in transforming a community and see more and more people find their way back to God. So most of the time it's been the results that have motivated me. And I like giving to organizations that will send me a letter and tell me how much my donation made a difference in someone's life. That just how it is in our culture, isn't it? We give because of the difference we think it's going to make. And it's a good thing to want to change things, fix things, make a difference, and see results. But should the results be my motivation?

Even though reward-motivated generosity and results-motivated generosity are natural to us and can be good things, they are different from the motivations God wants us to have for generosity. God has an entirely different approach to generosity. Check it out:

- *If you need wisdom, ask our generous God, and he will give it to you. He will not rebuke you for asking (James 1:5).*

- *"In that way, you will be acting as true children of your Father in heaven. For he gives his sunlight to both the evil and the good, and he sends rain on the just and the unjust alike" (Matthew 5:45).*

God isn't generous based on what he gets back from those with whom he's generous. God doesn't give based on rewards or returns; he gives regardless! God is simply generous with everybody, and Jesus told parable after parable where God is depicted as an employer who paid people more than they deserved for their work because he's generous.

In our lives we're either going to chase after the almighty dollar *or* chase after the Almighty God. When you chase after God, when you pursue God with your life, you become more like him, and there's no better way to be like him than to be generous. Have you heard that the basic tenet of biblical faith is that as human beings, we're made in the image of God (the "Imago Dei")? We're not God, but we were meant to resemble God, to reflect God. And I believe we're never more like God than when we are generous without expecting a return or demanding results.

God has all sorts of attributes we have no chance of achieving: omniscience, omnipresence, omnipotence. But there is at least one thing we can do to be like God: Be generous!

We often think it's human nature to be self-centered. But the Bible says something completely different: We were made in the image of God, and God is a generous giver. Generosity is our natural state, and it's only because we live in a world marred by sin that generosity doesn't seem natural and self-centeredness does.

So God is saying, "Be generous with others for one main reason: because I have been generous with you." Jesus explains it straight up: *"Give as freely as you have received!" (Matthew 10:8).* And Paul puts it this way: *You know the generous grace of our Lord Jesus Christ. Though he was rich, yet for your sakes he became poor, so that by his poverty he could make you rich (2 Corinthians 8:9).*

This isn't about giving more money and time; this is about giving in a different way, for a different reason, with a different motivation. We were in need. We were without. And God gave—generously.

I heard a tale of a church meeting where a wealthy man stood up and shared his testimony with the rest of the church. "I'm a multi-millionaire, and I attribute it all to the blessing of God in my life," he said. "I remember the turning point in my finances and my faith. I had just earned my very first dollar in business, and I went to a church meeting that night where a missionary told about his work and asked for financial support. I knew that I only had a $1 bill, so I had to either give it all or give nothing. So in that moment I decided to give that whole dollar to God. I gave all I had to God, and I believe God blessed that decision and because I gave all I had that's why I have what I have today." He finished talking, and a hushed silence fell over the crowd as he made his way back to his seat. As the rich man sat down, a little old lady leaned over to him and said: "I dare you to do it again."

I love that story. I want to dare you and challenge you. First, I dare you to give like God does—regardless of the result, unconditionally. Have some fun with it; we all have that person in our lives we don't want to give to because we don't like them or they don't like us, or because they are never really quite as grateful as we'd like. This week, do one generous thing for someone where you know it's not going to get the reaction you'd like to get. And when you do, say to God, "I want to be generous like you are. Make me generous like you, Lord."

Second, I dare you to grow in your generosity. I want this generosity thing to become a habit for you, a lifestyle. Not just something you do, but who you are. There is quite a bit of research that shows that it takes about 30 days to form a habit, so commit to practicing generosity at a new level, higher than you have before, for the next 30 days. And see if it doesn't start to become more "natural" for you.

We have been given the kingdom of God, and that kingdom is a kingdom of generosity because God is generous. Our God is generous without partiality. Our God is generous with the grateful and the wicked alike, and the King has been generous with us. That's our God! And this is our time to be like our God.

five questions

How generous or selfish are you or have you been in your life?

What do you think are the roots of your generosity or the lack thereof?

How does it make you feel when people are generous or selfish toward you?

Imagine Jesus tells you to sell all you have and give it to the poor; would you do it? Why or why not?

What opportunities has God given you to be generous? How have you handled those opportunities?

by Steve Carter

I have this friend who carries around an old vintage camera wherever he goes. We'll be hanging out at the beach, walking through some downtown, or just sharing a meal together, and he'll see something that cannot be ignored. At first I thought it was a little strange as I'd be mid-sentence and he'd start snapping away. I tried not to take it personally that I was never the central focus of his pictures, but I guess there isn't a huge market for people whose looks can be defined as a poor man's David Schwimmer.

If you were to see my friend Trever's photos, you would marvel at the way he is able to capture a moment. Recently, we were in Newport Beach, California, walking to meet our families, and he grabbed his camera and began shooting pictures of this old lifeguard tower. I started to ask him a plethora of questions that basically all centered on, "How are you able to capture such incredible images with that toy camera?"

Trever kind of laughed and then said, "It's all about light; great photographers are students of light."

Scientists will tell you that light is the primary source of energy for the universe, religion professors will tell you that light is one of the central images of many faiths, and photographers will tell you that light is their chief resource. The English word "photography" is the result of two Greek words that have been combined, with a literal meaning of "light writing."

Photographers are not just chasing the light; they're writing about it. They don't write with words, but with each click they're capturing the essence of the moment that they see unfolding before their very eyes.

Great photographers have no choice but to be students of light, students of how that primary source of energy chooses to break through into our world. What if as followers of Jesus we oriented our lives around the same discipline: to be a student of light, to be a student of how God's grace invades our reality, to be a student of the divine in the daily?

Most of us live unaware of the light that is all around us. We move from one thing to the next, often doing multiple things at once. We text and eat, we talk on our cell phone while walking to class or a meeting, and we find ourselves in a conversation with someone while thinking about what needs to get done by the end of the day.

We miss it.

We're distracted.

We're overcommitted.

We're simply too tired to look.

I'm tired of missing the moments of heaven invading earth. Watching my friend Trever's awareness of the world around him is so inspiring. Sometimes it's a magnificent crescendo of colors like a sunset, and other times it is as simple as a smile. Big or small, my friend is an addict of light. He lives a life with eyes wide-open, expectantly waiting to see God's beauty manifested along the way.

It is so easy to get caught up in the chaos, but spending time with Trever has made me realize the discipline and practice it takes to constantly be on the lookout for light.

Since the beginning of humanity, people throughout the Bible saw a connection to God in light. When the Scriptures begin in Genesis 1:1-2, this declaration is made: *In the beginning God created the heavens and the earth. The earth was formless and empty, and darkness covered the deep waters. And the Spirit of God was hovering over the surface of the waters.*

So when the world began, it was formless and empty. When something is both formless and empty, its nothingness can be quite chaotic. What's so intriguing is that the Bible tells us this: *Then God said, "Let there be light," and there was light. And God saw that the light was good. Then he separated the light from the darkness. God called the light "day" and the darkness "night" (Genesis 1:3-5).*

This is our creation story. The earth was formless and chaotic. God speaks into this chaotic nothingness four profound words, "Let there be light," and light appears. God sees that this light is good, and then God chooses to separate light from the darkness.

So God creates light from the chaos and then chooses to separate it from the darkness. As Christians, it is so easy to forget about the light—to neglect the light and spend the majority of our time focusing on the darkness we see in our world. For many of us, we've become jaded, cynical, and deeply judgmental toward others and even the church. Sadly enough, unlike Trever, who consistently searches out the light, I can easily find myself looking for the dark in things. Sometimes it's the choice of words someone used or simply trying to find something in another person that is wrong so that I'll feel better about myself. I have become quite good at missing the light, missing God's presence breakthrough because I'm too distracted. I remember reading *Velvet Elvis* by Rob Bell and being deeply moved by this statement: "Why blame the dark for being dark? It is far more helpful to ask why the light isn't as bright as it could be."

Even as the church, we are still a group of broken and fractured people. But the good news is that in the midst of our own chaos, our own emptiness, and our own brokenness, God is declaring, "Let there be light."

Let there be light in us.

Let's not become the jaded people that focus solely on tearing down others.

Let us be the people of light.

To do this, we must create space with the one whom John declares "is light" in 1 John 1:5. For some people, this is something that they do to check it off the list, but God is about ongoing relationships. God desires the kind of relationship that isn't just a five-minute prayer when you wake up, or just reading some verses in the morning (the key word is "just"), but about a conversation that continues throughout your day.

This is what God invites us into every day. God invites us to be aware of our environments. Throughout our day, let's be aware of our surroundings, expectant that there will be something that cannot be ignored and willing to risk by actually trying to capture that moment. Whether you're in class, at work, walking into a difficult conversation with a friend, or enjoying some solitude at the beach, God wants you to be aware of him.

God invites us to be expectant that he might have something in store that we never could have imagined. We can be expectant that God wants to break through in any moment to showcase his love, mercy, grace, and light through us. God invites us to be willing to risk stepping into whatever he might have for us. We often think about this in regards to massive movements, but it usually centers around the moments that God's Spirit is leading us to ask this question, pray for this person, or share our story with someone.

To be a disciple of the one that is called light, we must be aware of him, expectant for him, and willing to risk with him. May you be moved to awe and wonder as you go throughout your day writing about the light.

In what ways have you been or are a student of God in your daily reality?

What things distract you and keep you unaware of the "light" all around you?

In what might you not be as bright as you could be as a "light to the world?"

How has God invited you to be aware of him in the environment around you? Ask God to help you be aware.

In what ways are you expectant of God? Ask God to make you willing to join with and risk with him.

by Cam Huxford

Pointing and Staring Is Not Rude; It's Worship

I have been leading corporate worship gatherings for years now, and I've been trying to come up with a picture of worship that I can wrap my head around. A few years ago I read Harold Best's book *Unceasing Worship*, in which he paints a picture of worship, one of a continual outpouring of all that we are onto God. Best goes on and correctly asserts that "no one does not worship." We are all pouring our time, talent, and treasure onto something all the time. It's just a question of what are we pouring ourselves out onto. His picture reminds me of what Paul writes in 2 Timothy 4:6, when he tells Timothy: *As for me, my life has already been poured out as an offering to God. The time of my death is near.* Paul paints a beautiful picture of a total emptying of himself in outpouring worship.

That has been an extremely helpful picture for me, but honestly, right now I struggle with it. Here's why: I have devoted my life to worshipping God, but I don't feel the way that Paul must have felt when he wrote those words. Paul's words to Timothy are followed by this sentence: *I have fought the good fight, I have finished the race, and I have remained faithful (2 Timothy 4:7).* Have I fought the good fight? I don't think so. Not yet anyway. I'm not looking back on a life of outpouring, thinking that I have poured myself onto God like a drink offering onto a fire. However, I do resonate with Paul in that I am feeling emptier by the day.

Recently, I have had a different picture of worship sitting on the back of my retinas. It is an image that comes from John 1. The picture is of the radiance of the glory of God revealed and three men's responses to it. One man stands shouting with his arm outstretched and pointing. The other two follow the trajectory of his pointed finger and stare in bewilderment.

The following day John was again standing with two of his disciples. As Jesus walked by, John looked at him and declared, "Look! There is the Lamb of God!" (John 1:35-36). What do you think John was doing when he shouted "Look"? I believe he was pointing. So the first part of the picture is a man pointing at the glory of God, revealed in Jesus Christ. In this case, John the Baptist helps me make sense of a concept that I have always wrestled with. It is a phrase that we throw around all the time. We say that when we worship we "give glory to God."

What does that mean? Does it mean that we give him a little bit of our glory, that we share our glory with him? I don't think any of us are crazy enough to believe we are doing that, but when we use this phrase, it seems like that's what we're saying. I think that phrase "give glory to God" is better put by borrowing from King David's words in Psalm 34:3 and saying we "magnify the glory of God." John Piper makes the important distinction when interpreting David's words that when we magnify the glory of God, we do not mean that we make something bigger as if God's glory needs to be added to. That type of magnification, like what is done with a magnifying glass, would seem ridiculously unnecessary. However, a telescope also magnifies. The difference is that its job is not to make something small bigger. Its job is to take something that is so mind-blowingly huge that it cannot be comprehended with the naked eye, and make it visible to us.

That is what I think John the Baptist was doing when he worshipped in John 1. He magnified the glory of God by pointing at Jesus Christ. Earlier in the passage, John talked about his glorious object of worship, declaring that the Lamb of God would take away the sin of the world. What is bigger than that? What is more gloriously gigantic and incomprehensible than the Son of God becoming a sacrificial lamb in order to take away the sin of the entire world? I would submit that the two disciples who were standing next to John would have both needed mind diapers if they'd tried to wrap their heads around that truth. John magnifies something catastrophically big, what Hebrews 1:3 also reveals, saying *The Son radiates God's own glory.*

John points and says to look at the glory of God—it's Jesus. Behold it, even though you can't possible take it all in.

Notice what happens next from our passage in John: *When John's two disciples heard this, they followed Jesus (John 1:37).* When they heard what John said, they did what John said. He told them to behold and they beheld. He said look and they looked. As it turned out, they couldn't take their eyes off of Jesus, so when he kept walking by, they had no choice but to start following him. This is the second part of the beautiful image of worship that I see in John 1. One man worships by pointing; the other two worship by staring.

I feel this on Sunday when I am leading corporate worship in our gatherings. I think a lot about my role, and I think that the best I can possibly do is to simply point at the glory of Jesus and call people to look at it. We sing songs about God's glory revealed in Jesus, we preach sermons about it, we read about it in the Bible, and we beckon people to behold. Gaze into the glory of God. Worship him by staring in awe, wide-eyed and slack-jawed.

In speaking earlier from personal experience about my struggle with the outpouring image, I did not mean to say that Harold Best's picture is not a biblical one. I mean only to say that for me recently, I have a hard time with the "pouring myself out" picture of worship because most times I feel like I have nothing inside to pour out. I've poured my time, talent, and treasure on so many false gods in the past that I wonder if I have anything left. I'm not as much the drink offering as I am the empty cup. I come to worship totally empty-handed. But even in that pathetic state, my hope is that I can do what John the Baptist did and raise one of those empty hands to point at Jesus Christ. Thankfully, as I try to lift a weak arm, right about then I realize that by the grace of God, as weak and empty as I may be, my eyes haven't lost the ability to stare in wonder at his glory.

What has been your definition of worship as you've been serving God?

In what ways do you listen to or ignore those who point Jesus out to you?

How have you "glorified" or "magnified" God in your life?

How have you reacted to Jesus since he was pointed out to you?

In spite of weakness in your life, how are you pointing others to Christ?

by Jon Peacock

Busyness is a disease that surrounds us, infiltrating our culture and our campuses and infecting our lives. You see it everywhere, don't you? This busyness oftentimes works in our lives like the click wheel on an iPod Classic® or an earlier generation of the iPod Nano®. The busier you are, the louder your life gets. The louder your life is, the more difficult it is to hear God and respond to his leading.

I was just reminded of this as I watched a recent football game. The game was on the line; the crowd was going crazy. The quarterback walked up to the line of scrimmage and then began to make a gesture that was surprising. You might think that with the game on the line, the quarterback would want to have the stadium as loud as possible. However, the opposite was true. The quarterback waved his arms to let the crowd know that silence not volume was the key to victory.

How about you? The game is your life, and so much is on the line. Each day God has a purpose for you to fulfill. Each day God wants to download love into your heart through his voice so that you can live out his mission here on earth, on your campus, in your community, among your friends. When we look through the Gospels, we see that the life of Jesus looks quite similar to the quarterback with the game on the line. Jesus seemed to believe that silence and solitude are keys to victory.

It's hard not to be amazed at Jesus' lifestyle. While Jesus didn't have e-mails to answer, texts to return, status updates to check, tweets to scroll through, or finals to cram for, he had become a popular teacher with people clamoring for his attention, begging to be healed, longing to learn. It's a false assumption to think that Jesus did not have noise in his world. His pace of life existed within a culture that was trying to survive and thrive within the shadow of the Roman Empire. Despite all this, Jesus lived a life that was centered, a life that seemed to control the noise around him instead of being controlled by it. In Mark 1:35, Luke 5:16, and elsewhere, we see that he did this by practicing the spiritual discipline of solitude. His times of solitude reduced the noise around him so that he could hear from God the Father.

What comes to your mind when you hear the term "solitude"? For me, I think of boredom as a consequence that quickly follows. I'm an extreme extrovert, so being alone has never really captured my heart. So I've run from solitude for most of my life. I wish I could say that I'm an expert on this, but that would be stretching the truth for sure. However, solitude is something that is a more common part of my life now. Over the last few years, God has been teaching me that this practice of solitude is a catalyst for growth and impact. Most days I dream about God using my one and only life for great things, and most days I fail to see that "solitude" is a key for this vision to become a reality. Still, I've been striving to learn what Jesus knew: Getting alone and reducing the volume and noise in our world helps align our souls with God.

A buddy who is an expert craftsman recently told me over coffee that the most important thing in building is proper alignment. If the pieces, fittings, or walls are not lined up, then the finished product will be off. A home just a little off center will put anyone who enters it at risk. It's the same with us. When we neglect the alignment of our souls, it's possible no one will notice—at least not for a while. But eventually, we'll be off track and we'll wonder why God feels so far away. It's even true that anyone who enters our world might be at risk.

The spiritual discipline of solitude is a vehicle that can bring you into the presence of God where you can enjoy time and conversation with him. If a disciple-making movement is ever going to happen through you, then a solitude-choosing rhythm of life must happen first within you.

We see this rhythm of life not only in the life of Jesus but also in the Old Testament. Way back in the ninth century B.C. lived a man who was running for his life. The message of God and his purposes hinged upon this final messenger. At this point, it appeared that all of God's prophets had been killed, leaving only one remaining: the prophet Elijah. As you can imagine, Elijah was in dire need to hear from God. He didn't know what to do and wanted to give up completely. In 1 Kings 19 we see one of the greatest pictures of how powerful solitude can really be. The worry, anxiety, and fear that held Elijah captive to the point of despair were instantly unlocked by the power of a whisper. It was not in the noise of an earthquake, fire, or wind, but the stillness and quiet of a whisper that forever marked Elijah's life and the nation that he would continue to speak into.

So how about you? Does this story resonate with you? Are you one of the last ones standing for Christ and his kingdom in your community? The power to break through and impact is oftentimes found in the unpopular practice of solitude.

As you walk up to the line of scrimmage today, as the noise in your stadium reaches unbearable decibels, know that your key to victory is not found in more volume but in the quiet. As you choose to get alone with God, may his Word and his presence once again realign your soul.

On the last day, the climax of the festival, Jesus stood and shouted to the crowds, "Anyone who is thirsty may come to me! Anyone who believes in me may come and drink! For the Scriptures declare, 'Rivers of living water will flow from his heart' " (John 7:37-38).

If busyness is a disease, then when, where, and how does it affect your life?

If solitude is an unpopular practice, then how might its unpopularity keep you from developing this habit in your life?

What do you do to reduce the noise of the world around you so you can hear God more clearly?

How can you feel your life getting out of sync when you aren't hearing from God? What are the warning signs for you that this might be happening?

What disciplines have you created or can you create in your life to start hearing God more?

by Jodi Hickerson

A new frozen yogurt place just opened where I live, and I may be addicted already. It's unlike any ice cream place I have ever visited, and I would consider myself an expert in all things frozen treats. The thing that makes this place unique is that it's set up to be self-serving. You get your bowl—whatever size you want—and then choose your flavor of yogurt or mix flavors if you want. You can blend 10 flavors if you want; it doesn't matter—you make it how you like it.

Then you go over to the toppings and pile up anything you want on top. Graham cracker crumbs? You got it. Crushed-up Pop-Tarts®? Yes. Fresh fruit, syrups, chocolate chips, cookie dough, Sour Patch Kids®—you pick your perfect combination and then weigh it at the end to see how much your creation is going to cost you. Brilliant. I love it. I love knowing that every time I walk in, there are 10,000 different combinations that I get to choose from. Whatever I want. It's like the Starbucks® of dessert.

Honestly, I want most things in my life to be self-serving. I want to choose what I want to do, when I want to do it, and how I want every detail to go. Sometimes I live my life like it's all about me and I get to choose the perfect combination every day of what will make me the happiest. I'd like a little comfort, some security, mix in a little recognition, and top it all off with my timing, my desires, my schedule—and a little cookie dough.

I do this in my relationship with God, too. I try to just pick and choose what I want from him and leave out what's going to cost me too much in the end. I'd like to have God's grace, definitely need that. Also give me plenty of God's love, mercy, forgiveness, and protection. But getting out of my comfort zone, having my schedule interrupted, giving my stuff away, serving other people—that stuff just seems like it's going to cost me too much in the end.

But I'm learning that picking and choosing my perfect combination should be limited to lattes, frozen yogurt, and the occasional Extra Value Meal®. I'm learning that living a self-serving life is no way to live.

Jesus had some words to say about this, too. *"If you try to hang on to your life, you will lose it. But if you give up your life for my sake and for the sake of the Good News, you will save it"* (Mark 8:35).

If we hold on so tightly to our lives—our way, our desires, our plans, our comfort—we are going to miss out. When our primary concern is all about us and our lives and what we have going on, we lose.

We lose abandon for protection. We lose intimacy for security. We lose joy for anxiety. We lose peace for worry. We lose dependence for control. We lose faith for sight. We lose conviction for comfort. We lose the thrill of selfless serving for self-absorption. We lose risk for ease. We lose surrender for luxury. We lose generosity for storing up. We lose adventure for safety. We lose.

Yet somehow we have been duped into believing that we can find self-fulfillment without self-denial. Never happens. It's not how we were created. Jesus teaches that we will never find real life without denying ourselves, without laying our own way down.

And that can be tough, because I think if we're all honest, we want to get our way most of the time. We want a self-serving kind of life. But I'm discovering in my own life—and maybe you are discovering this, too—that freedom is found when I can give up getting my way for the way of others.

When we are able to lay down our entitlement, it frees us up. It frees us from our inflated egos, from our selfishness, our pride. And it frees us up to serve other people out of the most genuine place.

You see, serving others just naturally flows out of us when we choose to deny ourselves of always getting our way. Paul said that this was the attitude of Jesus that we should emulate. *Don't be selfish; don't try to impress others. Be humble, thinking of others as better than yourselves. Don't look out only for your own interests, but take an interest in others, too (Philippians 2:3-4).*

Choosing to put the needs of others above our own just has a way of nurturing humility in us. It's an inner working of our hearts that is only explainable by the hand of God. People that we used to envy, we now view with compassion. People we used to compete with, we now cheer on. People we used to pass by, we now notice. Things that used to annoy us so easily just don't anymore.

God uses service to grow our humility, and in our humility we choose to serve.

And we find life. Real living. Real fulfillment. Real community.

We choose to serve others not because it's the trendy thing to do, not because we might get a pat on the back or some recognition, not because they will then "owe" us, but because God has done a work in our hearts and we understand that our lives are not all about us anymore. And service that flows out of that place is the most genuine, the most fulfilling, and the most fun!

Think about what would happen if we applied that "you first" attitude to our lives and served one another in our homes. What if we considered others' interest above our own? What if we considered how another person's day had been? What if we helped others out, not looking for a payback? Having that kind of attitude? It could change a family.

But it doesn't stop there. Think about how living this out would impact your neighborhood, your workplace, your campus, your friendships. When someone is in need, we help. We pay for gas, we do extra loads of laundry, we mow lawns, we take the time to listen to one another, we allow our schedules to get interrupted. That kind of selfless service builds great relationships. When we are serving one another and putting each other's needs above our own, an amazing level of intimacy is built.

Think about how sincerely serving out of this place of self-denial would change your perspective on what you do with your money, your stuff, your time, your weekends, your vacation days.

Does it mean that we might not get our to-do list finished because we sat and had a conversation with someone that needed to talk? Maybe. Does it mean that we might not be able to buy that thing we want because we are helping someone out financially? Maybe. Does it mean we might not always get our way? Maybe. Does it mean that we might use our vacation days to take a trip to a Third World country and love on some kids? Maybe. Does it mean we might get snotted on in the church nursery? Maybe. Does it mean we might have to do the dishes? No. Just kidding. Maybe.

Whatever it is, we look to see if it might in fact be an invitation to live the life that Jesus led. The life he taught us about. And lay down our own self-importance for the benefit of others.

I want to live that kind of a life. I want an attitude of service that flows out of me. One that just quietly and unpretentiously goes around caring for other people. I want God to grow humility in me. I want my thoughts not to be about myself 99 percent of the time. I don't want to miss out. I want to find and experience the life Jesus was talking about. Don't you? It all begins with laying ourselves down.

I think I'm going to go out now for a latte and some frozen yogurt.

When have you adopted a "pick and choose" approach to the Bible? How has that affected your relationship with Christ?

Is it possible to find self-fulfillment without self-denial? Why or why not? Can we find self-fulfillment in meeting our own needs? Why or why not?

When was the last time you served out of complete self-denial? Was it tougher to find the answer to that question than it should have been?

How would your life change if you began looking every day for opportunities for self-denial?

What is one specific way today you can look to deny yourself and serve others? Go do it!